RISING SIGNS

by Carolyn R. Dodson

First Printing 1979
Second Printing 1982
Third Printing 1988
ISBN Number: 0-86690-034-9
Library of Congress Catalog Card Number: 82-71708

Published by:
American Federation of Astrologers, Inc.
P.O. Box 22040, 6535 South Rural Road
Tempe, Arizona 85282

Printed in the United States of America

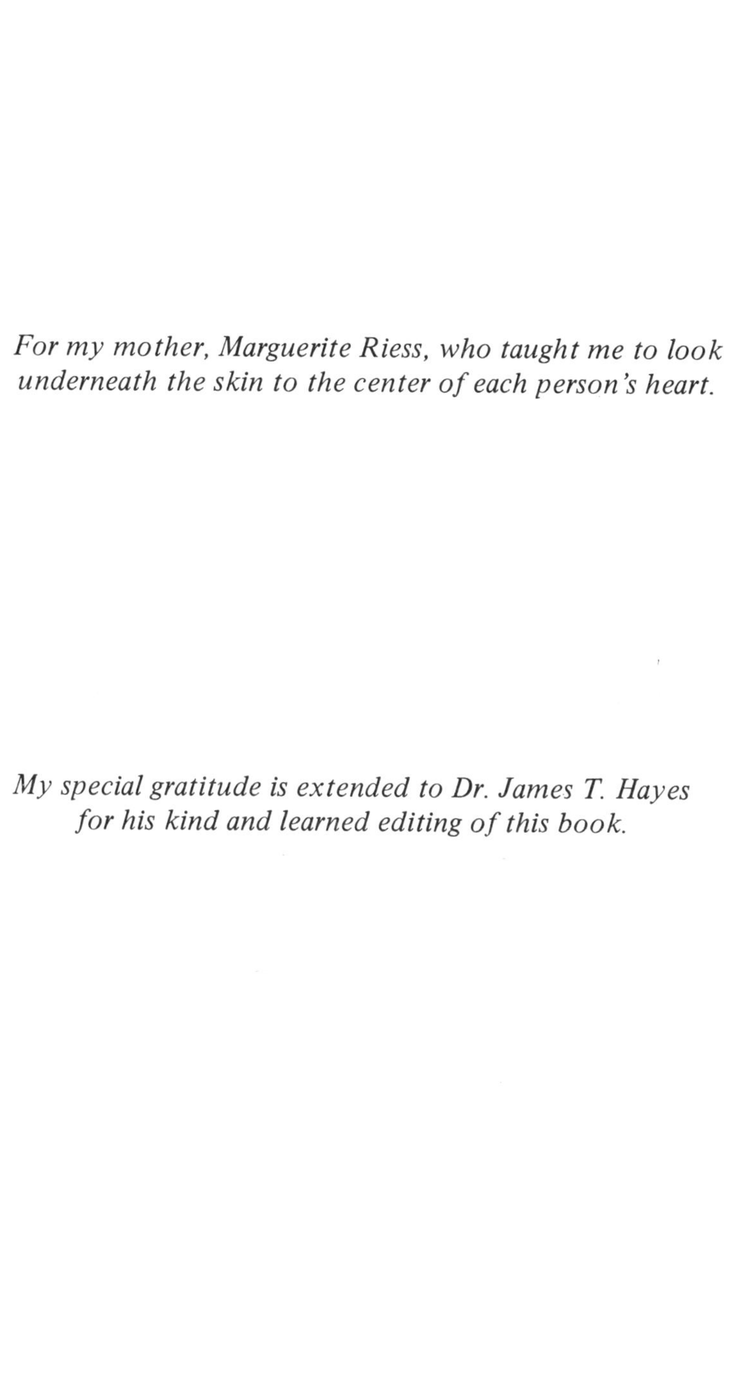

For my mother, Marguerite Riess, who taught me to look underneath the skin to the center of each person's heart.

My special gratitude is extended to Dr. James T. Hayes for his kind and learned editing of this book.

CONTENTS

INTRODUCTION

"You bug me". . . . . "holy cow" . . . . ."oh, horsefeathers!" Now really, do you think we're so far above the rest of the animals in our kingdom? If you have children, I'll bet they played on teams named for animals like "the Hawks" or "the Rams."

Our language is rich with animal analogies. When you say you're "as proud as a peacock" or "as mad as a wet hen", there's no need to explain further. These expressions paint vivid word pictures: all that's needed is one's imagination to create the scene of a strutting bird in his full array of tail feathers or a drenched chicken glowering from under the roost.

The signs of the zodiac are compared to animals or to human beings in a few cases for obvious reasons. Man evolved throughout history by both respecting and fearing nature and the animals that he encountered in his daily existence. The various expressions of nature were compared to an animal or to a human being that was descriptive of the expression.

A bull is a big, slow critter that chews on grass most of the time. He leads a herd of cows and calves and sometimes gets angry; then — watch out! A lion stalks the jungle and growls a lot, running all the other animals out of his territory, which he changes at his own whimsy. No wonder he's called the King of the Jungle!

Each of the animals should inspire similar responses in you imagination. It isn't necessary ever to have seen the animals to create the illusion in your mind. After all, the Chinese use a dragon in their astrology; and who's ever seen a dragon?

I wrote this book while living in a small, rural community in southern Kentucky. Many of the farmers plant by the signs and do not refer to each sign by its proper name, such as Pisces or Libra. Instead, they refer to the signs by their obvious names: the fish or the scales.

People whose livelihoods depend on nature have no need to use a name the root of which extends backward to a Latin origin. The "fish" represents sufficient symbolism to satisfy any agricultural or personal need.

The human symbols - Gemini, Virgo, Libra, and Aquarius - represent times when man must involve himself with his fellow man rather than perform tasks essential to his survival. Gemini asks that we join together with another. Virgo asks cooperation; and Libra seeks justice, law, and order. Aquarius asks that knowledge be disseminated to everyone, regardless of title. Although each of the signs represents a month of the year, the rotation of the earth every twenty-four hours brings each of the twelve signs into position on the ascendant for approximately two hours a day, creating the rising signs.

I chose animals to represent the four signs ascribed to human symbols in order to keep the patter flowing and to present alternatives to a symbol such as the virgin. Now, who wants to look like a virgin?

I don't mean to change a 5,000-year-old tradition in naming the swallow to represent the twins. Just keep the migratory bird pictured in the back of your mind while trying to describe the manner and habits of Gemini more clearly. Gemini-rising people really do bob their heads up and down as little birds do especially when ther're listening. (Remember, listening is a task for Geminians because they're geared to talk!)

Aquarius-rising people swoop down on ideas, carrying them to great heights while remaining elusive and solitary. I could never understand why the eagle was given a quasi-rulership over Scorpio instead of Aquarius. It is not that the rulership was ever official, but I had always hear that there were "low" Scorpions and "elevated" Scorpions who had somehow progressed beyond the vindictive nature of the sign. (As if the other eleven signs don't come in varying degrees of development!)

The Scorpion holds many virtues that can be emulated. I implore all Scorpions to look more closely into the virtues of their animal symbol. Certainly, the Scorpion stings; but have you ever been bitten by a horse? Have you ever heard of throwing the Christians to the Scorpions? Certainly not. Please keep your impressions logical and sensible.

We all look and act more like our rising signs than we do our Sun signs. The ascendant is the most sensitive point of the horoscope, taking on the celestial influences of the moment of birth. Sun sign astrology (the astrology columns found in newspapers) became popular when businessmen found a way to cash in on the idea. They established the method of describing people's traits according to their dates of birth, rather than using their rising signs, which would be more correct.

Using one's Sun sign makes it unnecessary to have a horoscope case to determine the correct rising sign. For this reason, Sun sign astrology became an accepted method of predicting future trends, no matter how general. A lot of misinformation still exists today because of shoddy writing on the part of journalists who are attempting to cash in on the astrological market.

I began picking out rising signs because I grew weary of well-meaning, but misinformed people who frequently asked me to guess their signs. I would say, "I don't know your Sun sign, but I'll bet you have Cancer rising." As you can imagine, their responses would be, "huh?"

Take the time to study your subject well and allow your mind to wander over all the possibilities. Listen to a person's voice and observe how quickly he moves around. Does he fidget and squirm and does he sit placidly? Does he interrupt? Does she primp and pat her hair? Do you wish he would brush that layer of dog hair off his slacks? How does he walk? What does he like to talk about? What kind of job does she have, and does she enjoy her work, or does she wish she could be off fishing by a lazy river?

How does she dress? Does she wear jewelry? What kind? What is his wife like, and how would you describe her husband? What does he do that really gets on your nerves? And when the chips are down, what are the gestures he seems most capable of giving or doing for you? How and where will he cop out? What's he all about, and what does he see in you?

These are some of the questions I attempt to answer in this book. If you have just met your subject, let your mind wander over all twelve possibilities and eliminate to yourself as you go along. It could go something like this: "No, it couldn't be a Virgoan because he hasn't mentioned work once yet in the twenty minutes I've spent talking to him; besides, the ashtray is spilling over."

"And it couldn't be an Arien, because he stopped talking when I interrupted, but it might be a Sagittarian. . . no, maybe a Piscean because he seems so involved with literature, or is it poetry he's quoting? He mentioned his trip to Europe . . . no, I think it's a Piscean because he seemed anxious when I mentioned the splinter in my finger, and he's already rubbing his own hand in the same place. I'd better get a few more clues. Say, do you like to fish? What do you think of Van Gogh?"

Don't let bias and prejudice stand in your way. For instance, if you're partial to Libra-rising people and you're trying to figure out a person you don't care for, don't exclude the possibility of Libra rising because you prefer to save Libra for people you like.

Be careful how you present these ideas to others. I'm still suffering in a relationship because I told a friend I thought she had Taurus rising because she looked like a cow. I meant it as a compliment, but she didn't take it as such. I think cows are beautiful. I love those big round eyes and gentle faces. Be subtle in you explanations and use adjectives that will flatter, not insult regardless of your innocent intentions.

I don't consider myself an expert on picking out and describing the rising signs of blacks; but through reading the mannerisms and characteristics special to each of the signs, regardless of race, you'll get the idea. Just as with whites, there are many sub-groups which differ within each other race itself.

You must also keep in mind tha national origins of people, regardless of their racial backgrounds. For instance, American blacks act, dress, speak, and move differently from the way blacks from the Caribbean Islands do.

Thank you to all the people whose faces went into this collection. Some of them didn't know why I was asking to photograph them. I quit explaining what I was doing because it sounded so incredible to most people who weren't into astrology. Many people didn't believe me, and others refused to submit their photos because of various suspicions or superstitions, and still others flatly disapproved of my motives. (None of the disapprovers were astrologers.)

Because each of us is unique, it is incomprehensible that one of these twelve chapters will fully describe a person. Despite the fact that I have been as specific as I could allow myself to be, I have had to modigy and to control my ideas to express my thoughts.

Don't pass up the pages that describe the CARDINAL, FIXED, and MUTABLE qualities. Likewise, read the characteristics of the elements of FIRE, EARTH, AIR, and WATER. As you will see, I have grouped the signs together by quality rather than have I followed the usual practice of grouping the signs by the elements. Each sign grouped under the quality has similarities in expression, as well as some common features of face, body, gesture, and mannerism.

Learning to recognize the different rising signs is one of the most pleasurable sidelights of astrology to me. I hope you will think so, too.

Carolyn R. Dodson

The ELEMENTS:

Fire, Earth, Air and Water

There are four groups of elements and three groups of qualities. Each of the signs has both an element and a quality, forming twelve separate combinations in all. For instance, there are a cardinal fire, a fixed fire, and a mutable fire. There are ARIES, LEO, and SAGITTARIUS, in that order.

FIRE-signs-rising — ARIES, LEO and SAGITTARIUS - people have a manner that speaks of adventure, courage, daring, and a desire to inspire others toward their ideals. FIRE people face life directly and go after the adventure of living.

Eyes gaze forward, full of fire to find the action. The eyes dance and play or burn with passion and desire. The nose is often the outstanding feature. Although it is more prominent on the faces of whites, it will be a little more prominent on faces of blacks, too.

FIRE posture is straight and bold; the stride is long and sometimes militant. Even mutable SAGITTARIUS leaps into life - alas, at times with an air of apology which is evidenced by the stooped or rounded shoulders.

Words are ejected from the mouths of FIRE-rising people in bursts and gusts, loaded with passion and emotion or filled with philosophical questions. Their thoughts are expressed with a broad range of modulation to dramatize the thoughts and feelings behind them.

EARTH-signs-rising — TAURUS, VIRGO, and CAPRICORN-people speak of stability and substance. They are often loaded with charm but may place their responsiblities and their wishes on a priority list, taking care of the have-to's, before the want-to's.

EARTH people are easiest to spot by their prominent skeletal structure which often endows them with outstanding cheekbones, broad foreheads, and solid jawbones. EARTH-sign-rising people face life with a knowledge and an awareness. It seems that they have more sensitivity in understanding mankind, taking for granted human nature and all its shortcomings.

Eyes gaze with awareness, comfort, and knowledge so in tune with life that they seem to know what will happen before it ever takes place. These eyes stand out in their comfortable glances and sympathetic gazes.

EARTH posture is solid; the walk is sure and firm with feet planted flat heel-toe in melodic cadence. The voice is deep or high, but words are spent with the reserve best suited to the cautious host or hostess. Though the voice may modulate when the topic is one of emotional content, it is more typically heard in soft, steady tones injected with lots of "ahs" and "uhms".

AIR people breeze in and out of our lives, touching us all with their thoughts and praises. They're not so inclined to inspire us as they are to share with us, to instruct us, and to enlighten us. In short, the AIR signs have a strong civilizing influence on mankind.

The warmth of the AIR signs is quickly felt in their quick smiles and friendly manners. You will easily be included within their circles for they aren't inclined to probe and to question your motives or your qualifications.

Words spill and tumble from their mouths as do the blowing breezes, interspersed with short gasps for air (what else?). At times, the summer breezes change to windstorms of heated words; but these flashes of turbulence quickly blow away to be replaced by balmy breezes once again.

I have compared each of the AIR signs to a kind of bird, as you will find under the individual chapters. In tradional astrology, each of the AIR signs is symbolized by a human being - proof positive of their earliest meaning as diplomats, arbitors, and guides in man's pursuit of culture and refinement.

WATER-sign people slip into and out of our lives to touch and caress us, to nurture and to weep with us. Their effect on us is not so vocal as it is felt within our senses. Sometimes these feelings are difficult for us to explain, and yet we know they are an important part of our existence. They are naturally nostalgic and often fearful of circumstances which seem to be beyond their control, particularly the Piscean, whose life is often dictated by circumstance.

Their giveaway feature is their deep, sensitive, and aware eyes. Despite a poker face, the WATER signs find it all but impossible to hide emotion from the windows to their inner selves.

Posture can be stiff and erect but may hide a soft, pliant soul within its framework. Often this softness is seen in the glide, slide, or tip-toe of the WATER step.

Words ooze out from between tight lips, but passionate phrases may crash and tumble like waves hitting a rocky shoreline. More often than not, you'll hear either their mumble or their infrequent bursts of frustration, for their words aren't words at all but are silent messages that you, the listener, must grasp.

The QUALITIES:

Cardinal, Fixed and Mutable

The quality of a sign defines whether the sign is CARDINAL, FIXED, or MUTABLE. This means simply that it is aggressive or over-bearing (CARDINAL), determined in its plans or stubborn (FIXED), flexible or wishy-washy (MUTABLE).

It is my opinion that the qualities of the signs bear more similarities than do the elements of Fire, Earth, Air and Water. Although I will refer to facial or body characteristics such as the "fire nose," the "earthy walk," the "airy manner," or the "water allure," I have found the characteristics of the qualities to be more easily placed into identifiable niches. Does he move quickly and with deliberation, or does he shift from side to side? Are his eyelids deep-set, round, and heavily lashed or insignificant compared to his smile? CARDINAL people lead with their noses, MUTABLE people are sometimes clumsy and don't watch where they are going (their minds are off somewhere else), and FIXED people plan each movement in advance.

How does your subject eat his meals? Does he grab a sandwich on his way out the door; or does he enjoy a predetermined meal, allowing plenty of time to enjoy it? Perhaps it's neither. Perhaps your subject holds the record for opening the refrigerator door and grabbing small bites. Learn the basic rules of CARDINAL, FIXED, and MUTABLE; and your investigation is under way.

CARDINALS move quickly, jump to conclusions, and snatch answers just to get the problem solved and out of the way. Their desires to get results sometimes force action before any solution has been thought up.

The nature of ARIES, CANCER, LIBRA, and CAPRICORN is to initiate action and to invoke response. Their motto is, "The shortest distance between two points is a straight line." There's no beating around the bush with these aggressive people, although among themselves their manners differ according to the element of fire, earth, air, and water.

Does she mosey right up and ask "Where have you been all my life?" She may insist that you take up her cause and there's no way out of it, so insistent is she.

All other indicators agreeing, the CARDINALS make good leaders and inspire the masses to follow. If there isn't a battle, they sometimes create one just to entertain themselves and their troops. Unlike the fixed and mutables, the CARDINALS enjoy action for the sake of action. They love contests and often have difficulty relaxing.

If there's a mountain to climb, you'd better believe one of the CARDINALS will be there, back pack in hand, to tackle the job. They have difficulty following through to the finish line sometimes, though.

Young adult CARDINALS are impatient to get right to the action of job or career and find it difficult to face the rigors of more schooling. They'll follow through when there's a chance to hop right into an existing position upon graduation - - a post they can count on. They favor careers which allow them to lead other people - their favorite pasttime.

As a rule, however, CARDINAL people have less formal education than do those with fixed or mutable signs rising. They require frequent reminders and encouragement in order to stay in school. They do their best when climbing the ladder of success from a lowly position upward toward the top of the heap and are unequalled at bragging on their accomplishments.

Likewise, they can run on praise and admiration but require it more often than do the other two qualities. Words are straightforward, direct and to the point. Even gentle Cancer says what he thinks straightforwardly, but he does so softly and with feeling. The natural restlessness and enthusiasm of the CARDINALS for all of life will help you in selecting the correct rising sign if there is any doubt.

FIXED signs move with deliberation. The nature of TAURUS, LEO, SCORPIO, AND AQUARIUS is to think things thoroughly through, taking action only when a conclusion has been reached. Their motto is "A rolling stone gathers no moss"; and then go on to prove that they like moss by applying themselves to only one thing at a time, to the frustration of those around them who are waiting for them to move on.

Their movements are slow, their actions deliberate, and their days usually planned well in advance. They cannot be rushed. Despite what appears to be a kind of chronic inertia, there is a dignity which pervades about them to soften the frustration you may feel at times in dealing with the FIXED-sign people.

Does he eat each meal sitting down, and would he rather skip lunch than to grab a quick bite? Does she insist that her third coat of nail polish must be dry before she finishes brushing her hair and it's nearly time to go? Are his features full? Are his eyes, nose, and mouth a little more "complete"? (I often say, God took a little mcre time in making the FIXED-sign people.)

These features stand out a little - - or a lot - - by longer, curlier eyelashes, an extra curl in the hair on whites and a fullness in the lips of all races. This fullness of features can be best described as voluptuous when exaggerated.

The steadiness of one of the FIXED signs rising will stand our best in decision-making and action which bears an element of importance. Sometimes these decisions actually take the shape of nondecisions. A good example of this is in one's decision against a divorce despite all the points in its favor. FIXED sign people have a tendency to get themselves into ruts and to stick with a bad situation rather than to face an alternative.

Each of the four FIXED signs enjoys the material side of life in its own way. Each savors food, attention, response, and relationships and signals its pleasure or approval with subtle body language. the FIXED-sign people seem to enjoy life a little more just because they take the time to listen, to taste, and to feel. The tenacity of the FIXED signs will help you in deciding on the correct rising sign if there is any doubt.

MUTABLE signs shift and sway as the wind blows, or so it seems. GEMINI, VIRGO, SAGITTARIUS, AND PISCES grasp ideas quickly but often have trouble hanging onto them. There is a softness of manner, yet a bluntness of speech, a special wit and charm (or an element of mania) about them; and sometimes it's difficult to get at the real person inside.

They excite easily and need to remind themselves not "to make mountains out of molehills." Their strongest suit is in fantasy-making and in inspiring others to look out, over, up, around, and through - toward a better solution. Although they may inspire you to look up, however, they may look downward toward the darkest possible outcome to their dilemmas. Don't worry; they'll be up again before long.

Unlike the Cardinals and the Fixed signs rising, people with MUTABLE signs on the ascendant sometimes seem to lack direction. They sometimes lack the ability to stay on a main course but can rekindle their interest easily and do so with apparent ease. Even tidy, punctual VIRGO may drive himself rather harshly at times in order to complete projects.

On the other hand, MUTABLES adapt quickly to each situation in which they find themselves but grow restless when they cannot grow, create, learn, and inspire. They nearly always make good students and have deep respect for higher education.

Does he recite authors verbatim instead of presenting his own ideas? Does he nod while you talk, as if to keep time with the rhythm of your words? He may then let his own words drift off in his response by cutting off his sentences in the middle as if he has become bored with his own thoughts and has changed his mind before he is finished with them. The MUTABLES chew their nails and doodle or drum their fingers and wiggle their toes and feet while they sit.

As in most other stop and start, shift and rearrange habits of the MUTABLES, their eating habits lack any sort of routine. They gorge and skip and pick in between times. They often leave things undone to be completed later on. This sometimes shows in their appearance, for their clothes may lack a button here and there, or the hem is out in a skirt or jacket, or they've forgotten to brush their hair.

Even orderly VIRGO may take care to button up his shirt collar while failing to see the gravy stain on his tie. They are gentle and poetic, witty, clever, charming and often artistic. They are inclined to weave spells so magical that you will scarcely notice their imperfections. The natural ambivalence of the MUTABLE signs will help you in selecting the correct rising sign if there is any doubt.

DECANATES

(DECANS)

A decanate, or decan, is one third of a sign, or ten degrees. The principle behind the idea of decans is that each sign is in its purist form at the beginning but takes on a sub-influence as it travels on toward the thirtieth degree. Incidentally, this principle defies the popular concept of cusps, or divided influence at the beginnings and endings of each of the signs.

Decans are always within the same element of FIRE, EARTH, AIR, or WATER. The first decan of a sign is always the same as the sign itself. For example, the first ten degrees of Leo is Leo; but the second, Sagittarius; and the remaining, Aries. If the rising degree of your horoscope were twenty-five degrees Leo, your rising sign is Leo; but there is a sub-influence from Aries. This sub-rulership may have a minor or a major influence in your physical appearance and your character. I have found sub-rulerships to be especially helpful in defining the AIR signs.

DECANATES (DECANS)

	FIRST	SECOND	THIRD
ARIES	Aries	Leo	Sagittarius
TAURUS	Taurus	Virgo	Capricorn
GEMINI	Gemini	Libra	Aquarius
CANCER	Cancer	Scorpio	Pisces
LEO	Leo	Sagittarius	Aries
VIRGO	Virgo	Capricorn	Taurus
LIBRA	Libra	Aquarius	Gemini
SCORPIO	Scorpio	Pisces	Cancer
SAGITTARIUS	Sagittarius	Aries	Leo
CAPRICORN	Capricorn	Taurus	Virgo
AQUARIUS	Aquarius	Gemini	Libra
PISCES	Pisces	Cancer	Scorpio

A REMINDER:

When reference is made to any and all of the signs, the reader must keep in mind that the author is speaking of the *rising signs*.

The CARDINAL signs:

Aries

Libra

Cancer

Capricorn

Cardinal   **ARIES**   **Fire**

ruler: Mars

Ariens expect to be ahead of everyone else. They slow down only when someone of higher authority like the law forces them to, but this happens infrequently. Now, who's going to tell an Arien what to do? He can be found where ever there's a chance to lead or to challenge or where he can be allowed the maximum amount of freedom.

Aries guys are able to make snap decisions, remaining opinionated, irrascible but loveable overgrown boys. Don't get me wrong; an Arien guy is proud to be a man and is fully equal to taking on tasks cut out for Superman. He enjoys flexing his muscles and may be found saving damsels in distress.

Aries gals are equal to their male counterparts in decision-making ability. They are inclined to carry more than their weight of responsiblity, taking on still more while everyone else in the crowd is edging toward the exit sign. Aries is long on courage and daring, short on patience and ability to endure indecision in others. Although he's labeled brave, she may be considered bossy or "libbish". Wise Aries gals usually learn to sublimate their directness to get what they want, thus avoiding the stigmas often tacked on about them. Both guy and gal Ariens set out to prove that geometrical axiom: "The shortest distance between two points is a straight line".

Aries is symbolized by the ram, or male sheep, best known for his grace and speed in gamboling over and around rocky mountain crags. He is admired for his courage and daring as he leaps headlong into space, landing safely on the narrowest ledges or as he dashes headlong across a field, stopping only to extract his horns from a tree trunk. Some oldtimers used to think that rams landed on their heads because of the prominence of their horns, which curve upward and backward. Rams do, however, lead with their heads.

Aries people were born to lead or to direct others; these qualities are evident in the body and especially in the face. There is a look of competent command and the ability to think swiftly, rightly or wrongly, making decisions that he or she will stand behind.

The Aries glyph is evident in the arched eyebrows, which hook up to a prominent nose bridge. The nose may be fat or thin or long or short; but the symbol will show in some way, even if the eyebrows are thick and bushy. The bushy eyebrows may appear similar to those of the Capricorn goat. The difference is found in the Aries brows and nose, which seem hooked together, forming the Aries "horns".

On others, there is a closer similarity to Libra than to the Aries features just mentioned because of the polarity of the signs. This is especially true with Aries gals; yet the arched eyebrows will always remain a prominent feature.

Rams have prominent noses that bulge between the forehead and the nose tip. This feature keeps them from hurting their heads more than necessary when they crash into trees and cliffs. You will find this feature on many Aries-rising people, too. Big, or slightly hooked noses project outward from the face. It seems, the bigger the nose, the more susceptible it is to being broken. This wouldn't be a problem if the Arien would think before he acts; but if he were to think first, he wouldn't be an Arien! Hook-nosed rams favor the world of trade.

On some whites, the nose is arrow-straight, extending directly down from the forehead. Rams with long, straight noses often take the lead in military life. Many other rams have small noses, displaying versatility of talent and the ability to either lead or to follow. Small-nosed rams lead more gently than do the other two types and are often found leading social types.

The chin is generally pointed, especially when the face is slender. Thin faced Arien faces remind me of arrows or blades, especially when those faces match up with arrow-straight bodies, giving the appearance of the sign's ruler, Mars. It seems the thinner the face, the more prominent will be the nose and depth of the eyes.

Eyes are deep set, showing lots of lid. Arien eyes appear fully aware of their surroundings, with a gaze as direct as an arrow's aim, yet passionate and playful. You'd better step out of the way once an Arien zeroes in on something he finds interesting. You may not notice the change in the eyes of your Arien subject because he checks over the terrain lightening swiftly, and blinks faster than a cameramen's shutter, mentally recording every scene within his view, no matter how distant.

Ariens clench their lips frequently and seem to be trying to keep their mouths closed. Many have thin lips that make this expression appear more prominent than it actually is. They often bite their lips or press them inside their front teeth in gestures of caution and determination. Sometimes the canine teeth extend beyond the front ones. There is also a tendency for Ariens to have capped front teeth, caused by mishaps when leaping headlong into space before they took the time to see where they were going.

Although rams seldom get a chance to wear beards or goatees (at least in the business world) they enjoy facial hair and will allow it to appear whenever they're away from the restrictions of home or job. When those whiskers emerge, they are left to grow here and there in wild disarray. Of course, Arien gals are attracted to guys who wear beards.

Hair is worn simply, with as much ease of care as possible. Gals sometimes wear it in a short, pert Joan d'Arc. Some Arien gals wear it long, shiny and straight, tied back for strenuous activity. Others wear it long and curly, or short and fluffy.

Guys are fussy with their hair, but it doesn't always look that way. Some guys treat their hair to cold waves and hair coloring. Because Aries rules the head, there will be a lot of attention focused to the head and a wide variety of possibilities should be apparent. Although most Arien people like to feel the wind through their hair and simply DETEST hats, others are CRAZY about hats. Some Arien guys tend toward baldness while still young but seldom cover their baldness with hair pieces.

Rams speak directly and enthusiastically, with determination and courage. They project words as if the words had been fired from a rifle or shot from a bow arrow-straight and aimed at a target. Because most Arien people are aware of this tendency - - - at least to a degree - - - they take extra care to speak more softly. But speaking softly or in full Arien style, the unmistakable voice of the commander can be heard.

Ariens come in two distinctly different body shapes. They are either as thin as a track star's javelin or they bear the physical characteristics of a gladiator - - short and stocky, with heavily muscled arms and legs. Because of the Libran polarity, many gals take on Venusian features, complete with an hour-glass figure. Arien gals often carry extra pounds in their thighs, even when they otherwise appear slim. Both

Arien guys and gals are capable of retaining a youthful appearance.

Some Arien people seem unable to put on an ounce; but others indulge themselves with unhealthy foods, adding pounds in those uncomfortable places - - the abdomen and buttocks.

Rams walk briskly and lightly, with a snappy click. They are especially graceful and lively on their toes and are often gifted in gymnastics. Because Ariens usually stand very straight, they appear taller than they really are. They run whenever they can instead of walking and prefer jumping over things rather than going around them.

Your first glance will show you the one who's in charge or who would like to be. Ariens push their way through lines at the super market or the theater and dash through stop signs and challenge everyone to whom they feel superior.

Ariens have places to go and thinks to do, and they don't like anyone or anything to stand in their way. Some rams act more like lambs and need encouragement to become the individual each was meant to be rather than to sacrifice themselves on the altar of another's pride and ego.

Ariens like to eat on the run; therefore, they grab food on the way out the door, stuffing it into the pockets and handbags. As a result, they are often junk-food freaks. They enjoy large breakfasts at the crack of dawn - they're early risers - coupled with a morning cheerfulness that will incite the ire of every morning grouch.

They don't care what they eat, but they'd better not have to wait any length of time for a meal or they'll eat the stale bread in the pantry and go on to other ventures. They stay slim and healthy on simple foods and a little medium rare meat, having sensitive digestive systems that are easily irritated by pressure from work and family.

Clothing is usually plain and uncomplicated, sometimes to the extreme of simplicity except for a few important buttons and buckles that will stand out as eye-catchers. Ariens enjoy wearing clothes that have a military look about them, preferring "fatigues" over full-dress uniforms.

They can be found in sporty but casual slacks and neat, well-tailored shirts. They wear jewelry that is significant for its meaningfullness but not for its beauty. Antique, commemorative and honorary pins may stand in lieu of medals of honor.

Rams are usually very athletic people. They enjoy a challenge for the sheer joy of the contest but often make poor losers. Although they enjoy brain twisters, their favorite sports are those that require physical exertion, courage, and a worthy prize at the end of the match.

Although their endurance wanes quickly, it soon reactivates, spurring the challenger on toward victory. Even when there's no one to join an Arien for a game or match, he will involve himself in activities that do not require any opponent at all, such as sports-car driving, hang gliding, or other solitary sports and activities. He enjoys going places alone and holds a secret desire for forbidden and death-defying, dare-devil ventures. There is a fondness for knives, and all sharp instruments.

An Arien avoids purchasing possessions that will tie him down to one spot. His love of freedom and the adventure of sailing in uncharted waters make personal property burdensome. He likes to own things, however, as long as he can throw them into the back of his sports car and take off at the drop of his Arien cap. He often considers children a nuisance and delays their arrival as long as possible.

Rams enjoy marriage for the balance and gentleness a partner can bring into their otherwise brisk and sometimes barren lives. They don't settle down easily and will fight off any fetters which restrict their freedom. Partners who are either trained or naturally endowed in a knowledge of the fine arts are preferred - - those who know the right people in the right circles and can go "straight to the top" whenever it's feasible.

Rams have deep emotional dependency needs, despite their ceaseless quest for independence. They need the security of home and family and to know in which plot their bodies will rest once thay have passed on. Although they resent authority figures, they seek the favors of those in high positions and bow dutifully to social and political leaders, hoping some day to surpass the positions of those they presently admire.

Ariens' most annoying characteristic is their tendency to butt in, giving their opinions when not requested. They have an answer for just about everything and seldom say, "I don't know". They leap into conversations, relationships, and just about everything else before they have thought out the consequences. Then, when they're thick in the middle of something that they don't fully understand or a relationship toward which they feel indifferent, they simply drop everything and run the other way.

Don't waste your words on criticizing Arien villains because they aren't listening. They detest nagging and despise interference from others. They're blunt beyond comparison, but they don't mean to be. They want only to get to the point and can't bear trivia or an ego trip on the part of somebody else.

Rams were born to lead with examples of the courage and determination they enjoy in great abundance themselves. Ariens are not flawless in character and seldom try to project such an image. Instead, they provide us with real-life examples of how they proceed despite the stumbling blocks in their paths.

Should you be loved by an Arien guy or gal, his love for you will grow as his respect and admiration grow. He will be headstrong and fiercely proud, yet capable of great abundances of love for one who will walk, or better yet run alongside, as he journeys through life.

<table><tr><td>Cardinal</td><td align="center"># LIBRA</td><td align="right">Air</td></tr></table>

ruler: Venus

Librans will do just about anything to stay in balance. Whenever the scales tip one way or the other, special words and actions must be initiated in order to get the scales back into balance once again. You will find these harmonizers anywhere that they can share their thoughts with others 50-50, creating a light, social atmosphere all the while.

Libran guys are at ease in meeting new people. Their enthusiasm is genuine, as a rule, for their personalities are expressed by their desire for an abundance of personal encounters. Your Libran guy needs to feel needed; he is often charming and debonaire.

These clues will help you determine the Libran gal as well, for she is affable, gracious, and charming. She's fond of meeting people and seeks outlets where she can display her social talents. Although you may find the Libran guy making a high pitched sale, you may find the Libran gal serving you your favorite cocktail or trimming your nails.

It's not the Libran guy and gal who is out of balance, it is our culture; and both he and she are reluctant to make sweeping changes on their own. They're not inclined to be deeply committed on their own, but they do enjoy backing others who will stand out in any crowd.

Libra is symbolized by blindfolded justice holding the scales that balance and weigh that which is of equal value, with those who are equally deserving. As in the other two Air signs, Gemini and Aquarius, a human symbol represents each sign. In keeping with the animal symbols of most of the other signs, I would like to replace the scales with the parrot as a symbol of the sign Libra.

The parrot is an ornamental bird, domesticated for its beauty and ability to mimic words and sounds. Its presence enlivens any social gathering and its attractive ornamentation graces the surroundings. Parrots often perch on one foot, stepping from side to side whenever they become impatient, especially when people talk to them in a repetitious manner saying things like "pretty boy!" They have wings but seldom get a chance to fly, at least in captivity. They are found even in the huts and dwellings of the natives of their own regions, for they enjoy the company of people and willingly submit to domestication. The parrot, like the sign I choose him to represent, is perhaps one of the most nearly human of all the animals.

Librans are among us to bring us together. They enjoy people for their differences and find something fascinating in each person they meet. For this reason, they are usually concerned about their appearances, for their handsomeness draws us to them more readily, and their light warmth makes us feel quickly accepted into their circles.

Most Libran physical characteristics are noticeably symmetrical, including the hair, which is often parted right down the middle. Quite often, the Libran nose has a gentle upturned bulb on the end. On others, one is reminded of the parrot's beak.

The eyes are soft, appealing, and active. They dart to catch each and every action going on in their surrounding area. Libran eyes are wide open, though, and easily express the mood of the moment. This look of surprise may remind you that the blindfold of Justice has just been torn away. The eyes show a lot of lid regardless of genetic origin. Eyes are deep set and gals are inclined to accent their eyes with alluring eye shadow.

In fact, whatever the fashion of the day dictates, Libran ascendants are more inclined than any of the other signs to display it. Eyebrows are gracefully arched and usually plucked to fine lines on gals. There is a neatness throughout the Libran appearance.

The mouth puckers easily to emphasize a point of conversation. Libran lips are often bow shaped and can be so exaggerated on some that they may remind you of a favorite doll or character from childhood. The mouth is sometimes difficult to pin down because it's almost always opening and closing. To say the Libran is a chatterbox would be putting it mildly.

Although the Libran smiles frequently, he is not likely to flash a toothy smile. He smiles sweetly with lips only partly open as he innocently blinks his eyes.

The chin is almost always pointed and fine. As a rule, the chin carries out the fineness and balance of the face. Now as I am writing of the fineness of Libran features, I can hear some of you saying , "Hah! Uncle Harry has Libra rising, and he looks like a truck ran over his face." I'm only asking you to look closely at the individual features and see that they are a little finer than those of most others.

Don't count on dimples to tell you that your subject has Libra rising! Although it does seem to be a more common facial feature, dimples won't be a decisive clue in your search for a Libran ascendant. Libran facial muscles seem to create a place for dimples alongside the mouth, however, which goes along with the softness of many of the other features.

Librans like to part their hair down the middle and to keep it neat, clean, and combed. Gals are more inclined to grow it long and let it flow than they are to pin it up. When that special social function is at hand however, she's sure to pin and drape her hair so that she will have the most alluring style at the ball, emphasized with elegant combs and hair ornaments. Libran gals also enjoy frequent hair style changes and may add to these styles and changes with the help of wigs and hair pieces.

The Libran voice is often light and breathy. The words seem to tumble out as if the autumn breezes have carried them on a cloud from Mount Olympus. Their manner of speech is magnetic and enticing. Some Librans, however, screech and cackle like jungle birds. There is some tendency to mimic words and mannerisms of others; therefore, listen closely for your Libran's own true way of speaking. His words are often sugar-coated, and he embellishes his phrases with an abundance of flowery adjectives.

The Libran body shape emphasizes the word "moderate" or "balanced." His is muscular, yet not he-mannish; and hers is often shaped like an hour glass. She has small, fine breasts and a slender waistline that is balanced by a pair of wider-than-average hips. His legs and arms carry out the general masculine appearance of a well developed muscular build, and her arms and legs are curvy and softly contoured regardless of any excess body fat. Otherwise, the legs may show just the opposite because sometimes the balance is more in terms of making up one place for nature's shortcomings in other areas.

Thus, if the torso is especially slight, the hips and legs will be especially stocky and solid right down to the toes. The waist on Libran gals usually remains slender regardless of body fat or other abundances and lacks. When the figure isn't obviously "waspish," however, then the abdomen protrudes, especially when the ascendant is in the Aquarian decanate.

Librans walk softly with a melodious clip, feet applied lightly but firmly. It may remind you of a ballroom dance step. They apply heal/toe and then spin partly around or step from foot to foot.

Your first glance will help you spot the Libran subject, for you will see a hint of the Grecian statue standing before you with a soft, gentle face and a body padded with a well-contoured layer of fat. This padding pertains more to gals than to guys; yet, the body structure of Libran guys will remind you of statues that have been chisled from stone. Of course, extra pounds will diminish these classic features, but vanity usually moves in to clear up any weight problem. The glyph of the sign's ruler, Venus, is a mirror in which the Libran can admire himself.

Libran eating habits often defy the most basic rules of nutrition. They're meal skippers; but they fill in the spaces by munching sweets, junk food snacks, and soft drinks. Although they usually drink alcoholic beverages in moderation, they favor sweetened mixed drinks and sweet wines.

At the table, they prefer light meals displayed on fine china, silver, and linen, detesting snatched meals in noisy unrefined hash-houses. A little salad, a bit of this-and-that, and dessert, of course, are always relished.

They pick too frequently at tid-bits of food and smoke to excess whenever they are nervous. They usually refuse to eat alone and are inclined to start diets frequently - - cheating on them even more often than not so that little is usually accomplished in efforts to lose weight.

Librans prefer clothing with a feel and look of softness about it: soft colors, muted prints and plaids, and neatly tailored shirts and sportswear. Dark or bold colors must be worn in extremely good taste. Should you find this ornamental bird in mismatched feathers, you can bet his personality and disposition will match his attire.

Marriage and partnership are as natural to Libran ascendants as are eating and sleeping. They are inclined to marry young, as well as more than once. They often feel incomplete without the nearness or knowledge of a loved one with whom they can confide and share each and every experience.

Loved ones should be prepared for a roller coaster relationship fraught with frequent arguments and dawn-busting discussions. This harmonizer is in search of a strong and able challenger who will also protect him from aggressors and who will make most of his decisions. A Libran seeks one who will open new doors to the "beautiful life" and favors one who will willingly pitch in and help with chores, finances, and entertaining.

Librans meet their security needs through their own personal recognition within their families. They hope to be talked about admiringly at all family gatherings and are often sensitive about their ancestral origins. Conversely, they strive diligently to please society as if they were appealing to Mom and Dad.

Librans are not overly active or athletic but will go along with nearly any game or sport as long as one of their favorite people is there as a competitor. Unless the chart shows a strong tendency toward a solitary life, a Libran won't be found any where alone, even if it's just to grab a quick cup of coffee at break time.

They enjoy sports that carry a lot of good manners and finesse about them, such as golf. Tennis is about as extreme an activitiy as a Libran is likely to enjoy, unless the chart shows a strong tendency otherwise, although football and other strenuous sports are desirable in youth for the instant popularity they provide.

Among their favorite activities is a fondness for light social chatter designed to help them learn more about people and to help themselves up the ladder of success. They don't often aspire to the top rung; they just want to be above the middle, among the "beautiful people." They enjoy debates and can be lifted out of a gloomy spell with a heated argument that will leave everyone but them exhausted and drained.

Indecision is the Libran's most annoying characteristic. He is also inclined toward shallowness, vanity, and insensitivity. Most Librans are somewhat indolent, and many are downright lazy. Many Libran gals consider housework beneath their talents, expecting "hubby" to foot the bill for domestic help.

Libran guys often leave a trail of clothing all the way to the closet door but wouldn't think of stooping over to pick it up and put it away.

Librans are determined people when they decide to help their friends get ahead and enjoy knowing people in high circles. Don't be surprised if you are suddenly dragged across the room by your Libran friend chattering, "You've simply GOT to meet Charles, he's just the person you've been looking for."

Librans are honest, fair and usually sincere in their efforts to make our lives more pleasant. They only pry into our personal lives to see whether they can help make it brighter. They enjoy entertaining us and are quickly forgiving after any sort of difference of opinion.

Librans were born to share all they have with us as long as we cut the responsibilities right down the middle. They will go a long way in doing what they can to keep the relationship going, but they can be driven away by too many demands. They're easy and tolerant about criticism - - all things considered - - and are willing to alter bad habits as long as they don't have to bear more than fifty percent of the blame. But when a Libran loves you, he expresses that love with all the romance, roses, and violins of a nineteenth-century novel because love, romance, and eventual matrimony are what Librans are all about.

Cardinal   **CANCER**   **Water**

ruler: The Moon

Cancerians need to be nurtured and protected from the harsh forces of life. They often take the responsibilities of others upon themselves by nurturing others, too. Whenever life becomes too difficult to bear, they retreat until the feeling of security takes over once again. They can be found anywhere that they can care for or guide others with sympathy, understanding, and love.

Cancerian guys are instinctively aware when things aren't going right with those around them. They can quickly adapt as wife and mother when they need to and seem to have a built-in talent for housekeeping. Don't get the idea that this guy is a Mamma's boy or a sissy in any way because he is adaptable to nearly all situations and is especially gifted in business ventures. He is adept with figures and can be found operating at the house of finance or guiding the bulls and the bears.

Cancerian gals are at home in the home but are equal to their men out there in the world of trade. Don't think the she-crab is any better adjusted to her role than is he, 'cause it just "ain't" so. In fact, guys are freer to seek both the outlet of the business world and the pleasures of caring for the home, but gals are torn between their traditional roles in the home and a career.

Cancer is symbolized by the crab, which lives in or near the sea. His body is covered with a hard shell that he carries with him at all times to protect him from the elements and from other animals. Sometimes, as in the case of the hermit crab, he inhabits the shells of other sea creatures, fighting with other crabs for their possession.

The crab's maturing process takes on many stages, each strikingly different from the others. Despite the insulated manner in which crabs run hiding inside their shells, they're aggressive little critters that will fight to the point of having a claw torn off. Fortunately, the loss is a temporary one; and a replacement claw soon appears. Watch the habits of crabs for yourself sometimes and see how they cautiously peek out of their holes and then scurry toward the ocean's edge, scurrying back once again to their holes by the water's edge.

Crabs can't bear to miss a single thing. There is a multitude of predators out there waiting to snatch them up. Their eyes are never still as they watch front, back, and side to side for any hint of an advancing enemy. So it is with people who have Cancer rising. They peek around corners and over books and newspapers, making sure the coast is clear before they proceed. Cancerians look with helpless sadness begging to be taken in from the cold. Even when laughing, those eyes retain a touch of melancholy.

Cancerians sometimes have round faces. When this is the case, the cheeks are full; and the chin bulges just a little, turning up toward the lower lip. More often, however, the Cancer-rising face is sallow and may even appear suken in the cheeks underneath the prominent cheekbones. Many she-crabs have heart-shaped faces with little lady-like noses.

Moon-faced Cancerians often have pugged noses. Bony noses stand out on sallow-faced crabs with the high cheekbones. Some he-crabs have noses with bends and bumps in them, showing the scars of scraps which ended in lose or draw.

As in all the cardinal signs, Cancerian eyelids are prominent. They show up even more because the eyes are relaxed and distant, evincing a hypnotic effect on others.

Crabs have soft and fully contoured lips. There is a special emphasis on the lower lip, which protrudes slightly, forming a pout. Whether or not it's pouting, the mouth is usually relaxed. The crab may form words as he listens to other people,

although remaining silent or whispering his responses while others ignore him or remain indifferent.

The crab often smiles with his mouth closed; thus, you may not notice the crab's teeth at all for quite a while. Instead, his smile is a sweet, gentle upward curve of the whole face. The mouth droops just a little at the corners because the crab often looks at the dark side of life. He is equal to a grin, however, and enjoys being teased almost as much as he loves being loved.

The Cancerian chin is square and long on sallow-faced crabs. On some others, the chin protrudes and may confuse you with the chin on the bull. Still other crabs have pointed chins with the entire jawline drawn up into the contour that appears to start just below the ears.

The crab's hair can be silky and soft as the ocean's foam or as course as dry sea weed. It is especially vulnerable to the individual's health. vitamin deficiencies show up quickly, as will any sort of long-term stress. Whites tend toward black hair that grays earlier than it seems it should and is more inclined toward wiriness. Guys aren't shy about sporting toupees, and gals favor wigs and drastic hair color changes.

Words are spoken softly but quickly with a charge of emotion or in a shrill, pleading whine. Crabs laugh with a crash and tumble the way the ocean's waves spill and roll across the beach. Their tones of voice and manners of speech are highly susceptible to their moods for the moment: soft one minute and aggressive the next. Crabs are often seen mumbling to themselves and like to imitate accents and speech patterns that sound funny to them.

The Cancerian body shape draws attention to the stomach area where all excess fat is stored. This storage pouch is carried high and can easily be distinguished from a Virgoan abdomen because of the difference in height. The drooping shoulders may cause a slouch that adds to this slightly (or greatly) protruding abdomen even when his appears well developed.

Gals may or may not have large breasts. It seems that either her breasts are rather large or that she is flat-chested. She is conscientious about her bustline and is more inclined than her sisters of the other signs to have silicone implants.

The crab waves, points, and gestures in efforts to get his point

across. He is inclined to snatch and grab at something he wants to see. Some have hands and feet that are noticeably fine and small; but on most others, those hands and feet are large and bony.

Cancerians walk with a sideways step that may appear to be pigeon-toed. They seem to walk as if they were strolling on the beach and are happiest in or near the water, doing best of all on sandy surfaces where others flounder.

Cancerians are concerned about their appearance and seem to change it more often than do others. Some days they look like polished jewels, but their appearances on other days suggest that they should have stayed inside their shells. The extremes of appearance are greater; therefore, don't be surprised if that gorgeous gal next door suddenly shows up with stringy hair and face cream. She's only preparing for her molting stage, which, when complete, will bring her to a new level of appearance.

Your first glance will show you the restless creature whose emotions may sometimes control him. He may fidget with his hands, pace the floor, or walk the streets of a sleepy city in the wee hours, thinking and planning while he walks off an uneasiness he can't explain. He may never find the answer but the problem usually disappears quickly only to be replaced by another. He may be susceptible to the Moon's phases and may enjoy staying up late at night watching old movies on television.

Cancer-rising people invented the snack. They prefer eating small portions frequently, but the crab's snacking appetite can become uncontrollable at times. Anxiety may produce noshing attacks which make it necessary to move the bed and bureau into the kitchen (or the refrigerator into the bedroom). Sweets are a constant lure and a Cancerian shares with his fellow water sign people the temptation to imbibe in excessive amounts of alcohol. Dieting is nothing short of a painful experience unless it includes generous portions of wine and cheese, the crab's favorite foods. Cancerian guys make excellent cooks, not to mention Cancerian gals. It's their natural instinct.

The crab enjoys wearing casual clothes that fit loosely or give him freedom when he moves. He prefers soft, supple fabrics; but she'll endure a stiff gown if it's shimmery and glimmery enough on special occasions. Most of all, the feel of the fabric takes precedence over design. The nautical look always holds top honors in the crab's closet.

Cancerians are fond of all water sports, and are usually natural sailors. They aren't wild about competition but once committed, will fight gallantly to the finish. They prefer challenges when the odds are clearly in their favor or when there is a friendship, a romance, or a business deal to be gained at the end of the match.

Young male crabs may fight their ways out of the ghetto by proving their worth in the boxing ring. In fact, all Cancerians are fascinated to some extent by brutal bouts but usually prefer to remain spectators. They prefer to know the odds before the match and take a loss as a personal mark of failure.

Almost all crabs seem to have a special knack with wood, making excellent carpenters, wood crafters, and printmakers. They love to know what's going on in their circles and spend lots of time on the telephone exchanging gossipy tid-bits. They enjoy buying and selling and make good tradesmen, in everything that's for sale. The crab is a natural wheeler-dealer.

Cancerian restlessness and changeability imply some discontent with a single mate on a continuing basis. The partner is often a mother or a father figure. Whomever the crab chooses for a mate, you can bet his or her mother approves. The best choice a crab can make in marriage or romance is to choose one who is steady and solid. He needs one who will allow the crab room to shrink and to expand at his own rate but who will still provide a home and an abundance of security. Nonetheless, the mate must be prepared to step in and to take over whenever the seas become stormy.

Cancerian security needs are met best of all when he is well accepted by those he loves and respects. Because he is so easily threatened, he finds comfort in those who accept him just as he is. He seeks personal independence and harbors hope that someday he will be able to make all his own decisions - - an accomplishment he struggles daily to achieve.

The crab is sometimes a nagger and a faultfinder, expecting everything to be done his way. He can get totally steamed up over an issue, turning lobster red from head to claw. His passions often lack reason, however. He must allow room for logic and common sense to enter his opinion.

Crabs are sometimes excessively nosey as they peek through curtains or around doors observing everyone who comes into and out of the apartment house or the neighborhood. They're quick to pass on the latest bit of gossip, exaggerating and coloring the information so convincingly that the stories are often difficult to dispel. Cancerian insatiable curiosity makes crabs excellent newscasters, however.

These Moon-ruled children have spells of being crabby and moody. At these times, they need to be left alone until the tide goes out. They may see all sorts of opportunities in other regions of the country or world, but they are likely to feel too responsible or dependent on their families ever to take advantage of them.

Crabs can't relax; and when they try to sit still, they fidget and squirm. It's difficult for Cancerians to remain silent for very long and nearly impossible for them to keep out of other's businesses: unthinkable to remain indifferent whether or not an opinion has been requested.

The crab wants only good to come to all those whose lives he attempts to manage. He can be labeled a "busybody'" but never can he be accused of cold indifference. Even if you don't do things his way, you'll quickly be forgiven if you show you're steady and reliable.

It's a cold cruel world to a Cancerian, and he works hard to warm his surroundings no matter where he finds himself. Crabs are also highly susceptible to criticism; therefore, if you're planning to cite Cancer's faults, choose your words carefully with plenty of love for good measure; that is, if you don't want a pincher planted firmly in your thigh!

Cancerians were born to care for you and to nurture and to help you in your moments of loneliness and concern. They may never come right out and tell you how much they care because they're clumsy with words sometimes. Instead, a Cancerian will make a home for you, complete with a warm meal and a soft pillow. And if you're lucky enough, your head will lie snugly next to your Cancerian love.

Cardinal   **CAPRICORN**   **Earth**

ruler: Saturn

Capricorns need to feel important and socially acceptable. When there's no opportunity for advancement, they may fall downward toward temporary depression until the faint glimmer of success looms once more on the distand horizon. You will find these climbers in all areas where there's an opportunity for self-improvement -- whatever the words "self-improvement" mean to each Capricornian individual.

Capricornian guys are able to recognize the opportunity ahead of them and then to grasp it as they succeed in either business or politics. (It's not the type of profession that matters, for Capricorn men will go into any profession which promises success and recognition.)

Gals are achievers, too; and they are capable and well respected in the business world, for they are known to be decisive and challenging. Many other Capricornian gals, however, seek recognition through their husband's or father's achievements, thus rewarding themselves as civic leaders through association. Both guy and gal Capricornians are go-getters and are happy only when they feel they've risen above the multitudes. Should a Capricornian resist these natural urges to climb the highes mountain like Yertle the Turtle in the children's story, however, he may plummet to cavernous depths. In fact, it seems great depths and ever greater heights are preferable to the wide spaces in between, for these mountain climbers see no advantage in mediocrity.

Capricorn is symbolized by the mountain goat that leaps around perilous mountain crags where most other animals would fear to tred. His sturdy legs and rubbery, sharp-rimmed hoofs make it possible for this beast to cling to the most difficult slopes, enduring the tearing storms and bitter cold.

At hint of any sort of danger, the mountain goat instantly leaps upward toward his domain at the top of the mountain, which to him alone is a castle. His existence is a solitary one. But for small family groups, goats have no herding instincts.

Oldtime hunters claim the goat is vulnerable to capture only when approached from above.

Goats are built to withstand the rigors of personal denial and to enjoy the sweet, sweet taste of success when they are victorious. Therefore, a panoply of extremes is evident in people with Capricorn rising, particularly in the face.

High cheekbones stand out on Capricornian faces as if they were mountain cliffs. (Don't forget to consider that your subject may have Cancer rising, the polarity of this sign, which quickly picks up reflections from across the zodiac.) Capricornian high cheekbones are a dramatic feature, and usually a handsome one, too.

Like the prominence of the cheekbones, the Capricorn nose may protrude straight out from the face, reminding one of a plowshare that tills the soil. Goats approach life directly, and their noses often lead the way.

Because the bone structure is such an outstanding feature, in Capricornian people, the forehead will also be prominent. It doesn't usually cover a wide expanse as does the bull's but rather projects forward, or so it seems, as if to shelter the eyes from some of the harsh realities of life.

Eyes are set securely underneath the protective forehead. They are deep set, revealing lots of lid as in all the cardinal signs. Those eyes are seldom motionless, although much of the time their movements are very subtle. At other times, the goat observes easily, as if to scan the distand horizon from a vantage point atop the highest hill around. There is always an awareness of the pitfalls of life, in the goat's eyes. Even when happy, the goat smiles from the nose down. Those sober eyes remain cautious and watchful and always look just a little sad.

Regardless of the race or genetic background, goats nearly always have thick, bushy eyebrows. In fact, they take the prize in eyebrow size, winning over the ram, the brows of which are thick and bushy but usually arched. Capricorn eyebrows seldom arch without the aid of tweezers and often grow all the way across the forehead without pausing in the middle over the nose.

Goats have full lips that are firmly set. Even though they smile often, the lips are usually tense and controlled.

I have found a tendency for Capricornians to have broken or decayed teeth. On others, teeth are crooked; or there are gold teeth to replace those lost from spills and falls. Many goats have beautiful teeth however, whether or not they're capped. There may be a wide space between the front teeth, a trait that can also be found in the Capricornian decanate of both Virgo and Taurus.

A Capricorn is very much involved with age. While other children play with abandon, Capricornian children are serious and responsible by comparison. As the years mount, however, the tables gradually turn and the Capricornian enjoys youth while others are complaining about their social security checks. Capricornians are old when they're young and young when they're old.

This involvement with age -- which the goat compares to wisdom -- tells us that it is not uncommon to see wrinkles on the still-young Capricornian face. She'll be giving up some of the "ribbons" she's earned in her struggle to arrive at the pinnacle of wisdom and maturity she now inhabits should that Capricornian gal seek a face lift.

Goats wear their hair in simple fashion or extreme neatness and efficiency or extreme high-fashion noticeability. Guys, as well as gals, pay high prices for hair coloring, cold waves, and other articificial aids. Capricornian gals who wear their hair long wear it REALLY long; and when they wear it short, it's REALLY short. Gals enjoy piling their hair on top of their heads with every curl and twist in perfect order.

The Capricornian voice is usually soft and deep under normal circumstances; but when excited, he will zoom the voice upward in dramatic tones and then downward to dramatize the point. The goat will plead, gesture, and often attempt to intimidate his audience with commanding tones and words, especially when he has "been there already" and knows what mistakes can be made.

He doesn't like to repeat his words; therefore, you'd better listen carefully the first time. Capricornians are cautious about what they have to say and will tell you just enough of a gossipy tid-bit to whet your appetite. They're not about to disclose incriminating details because they don't want to be held accountable. They make great politicians.

Capricornian body shape, when unencumbered by extra pounds, will often appear very muscular and well developed. Goats don't need to work hard or to exercise in order to develop their musculature, either. Yet the body appears capable of extremely hard work and endurance. Many fine ballet dancers have Capricorn rising.

When life becomes dull and boring, Capricornians tend to add extra pounds, but still other goats can't seem to put on an ounce. Hands often bear the marks of toil in prominent knucles and bony fingers that show the struggle they endured to get where they are. Fingernails are sometimes stained from soil or grease or of the earth itself.

The goat walks on the balls of his feet with his heels resting after. There is a clip to the goat's gait – sure but quick. Capricornians like to hear their heels click as they walk and they walk with authority.

The goat usually has punctual and well-disciplined eating habits. He needs to eat often as a rule, for he burns up his food quickly. Should the goat decide to fonder, however, he does so with determination enough to convince us he's working at it. Conversely, he is the most capable of all the signs to adhere to a strict diet. Where booze is concerned, goats may abstain for long periods of time because of health or religious reasons and then plunge head long into the barrel in a "lost weekend," only to emerge with vows of abstinence once again. The sign is seldom known for moderation, to say the least.

Capricornians prefer simple meat-and-potato meals -- nothing fancy. But they are clever at putting on a prize winning spread when the boss is coming to dinner. In fact, they excel at nearly everything they do, or they just don't bother to do it at all. They are excellent cooks but usually don't like to waste time cooking and cleaning up when there's work to be done.

Goats wear clothing that describes their professions. They are most often seen in conservative business suits but are equal to any occasion, any time, any place. If she decides to wear her neckline in a low plunge, you'd better believe it will PLUNGE. She can be a tempting siren in the evening, returning to a prim and proper schoolteacher the next morning, fully equipped with a high-button collar and horn-rimmed glasses.

He's equal to the same extremes as is she -- kaftans and beads away from the job but gray flannels at the office. Goats sometimes wear dark glasses indoors as well as out to either avoid recognition or to tone down the harsh realities they perceive in their surroundings.

Capricornians enjoy strenuous sports when they know they

are capable of winning the match. In whatever endeavor the goat involves himself, he fully intends to win and will accept second place with grudging submission. Their competitors must be prepared to be intimidated and psyched out. Should the goat recognize his foe's superiority, he will make it a point to play badly, drawing attention to himself in his poor style and stupidity. Either way, it's his intention to bump you out of his path toward the top and then to rise above you. Should you have proven your superiority in the last match, chances are your goat-opponent is practicing up for a rematch -- for a time when he feels he's going to prove himself to be better than you. Most activities revolve around his desire to achieve; therefore, work can take up to nearly all the goat's waking hours. They take their work home from the office or have an office at  home. They like to own their own businesses and especially enjoy giving orders to subordinates.

A Capricornian seeks a marriage partner who is soft and vulnerable to him while he feels capable of handling the problems and all the tough stuff. Because the goat sees life as cold, lonely, and filled with bitter memories, his mate must be soft, gentle, and capable of expressing emotion.

Goats are not inclined to be sentimental and find amusement in others who save memorabilia. Sometimes their digust for anything but useful things includes people, too, for friends and loved ones must prove useful and worthy to the goat, who is carefully plotting his ascent through life.

He is nearly always a reliable parent, taking his offspring's material and emotional well-being very much to heart. (A Capricornian ascendant person is often one whose childhood was marked by the death or abandonment of a parent, leaving the kid a mountain of responsibilities.) His security needs are based on his own ability to surmount any problems which might arise. He learned very early in life to depend on few, if any, people except his own family; and sometimes even they are a disappointment to him.

Capricornians expect to know important and influential people in high places. Although they often feel ill at ease in fancy situations they willingly submit to stiff collar or stockings and girdle to attend formal functions. It doesn't take them long to learn which fork goes with which course at dinner or to imitate phrases and speech patterns of those they respect and admire.

Goats are quick to criticize sloppy work habits, tardiness, and ineffiency. They are also quick to criticize those who would flash fancy degrees from fancy schools, instead of proving personal competence through personal effort and experience. The goat learned the steps of his profession by climbing up the ladder to success carefully, step by step.

Each takes pride in his humble beginnings and may even brag on it. He may be cold and calculating in personal encounters, using his friends and relatives to help him get where he wants to be. Yet he may be coldly indifferent to his own friends and relatives who plead the same special favors. He is coldly decisive and indifferent to many around him until his position is secured at the top of the heap.

But they were born to lead society out of the murky depths of emotion -- upward toward logic and reason. Capricornians seem prepared from birth to bear the burdens of society, and especially those of their families.

Although you may not feel a strong sense of love for your Capricornian friends and loved ones, you will feel gratitude and appreciation for their efforts, and mostly for their rock-solid stability. But if you have reached inside to discover your goat's pliant heart, his responding love may set records for new heights; for his need for close, personal relationships is intense, and he may love you with abandon.

The FIXED SIGNS:

Taurus

Scorpio

Leo

Aquarius

Fixed **TAURUS** **Earth**

ruler:Venus

Taureans have to be prepared before they make a single move. They like to know the odds before they get into things. They're tender and affectionate and need plenty of lovin' to keep them happy and healthy. You will find these gentle but stubborn lovers of beauty and comfort any place there's a warm atmosphere, a soft chair, and a bountiful spread on the table.

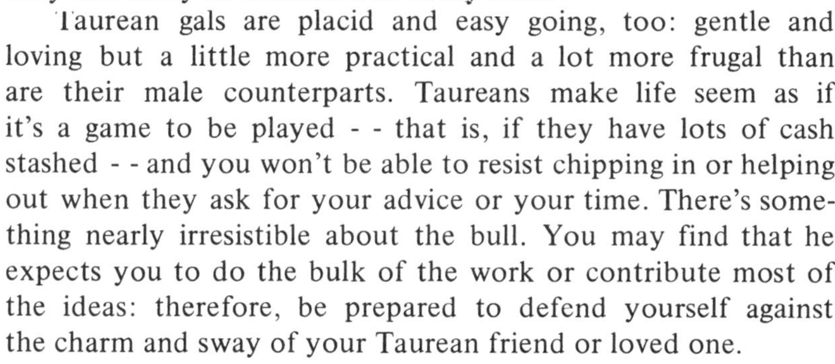

Taurean guys are friendly and comfortable to be near. They are able to spot a beautiful woman from a hundred yards away and like to be seen with one on their arm. They're soft and cuddly: they can easily be described as teddy bears.

Taurean gals are placid and easy going, too: gentle and loving but a little more practical and a lot more frugal than are their male counterparts. Taureans make life seem as if it's a game to be played - - that is, if they have lots of cash stashed - - and you won't be able to resist chipping in or helping out when they ask for your advice or your time. There's something nearly irresistible about the bull. You may find that he expects you to do the bulk of the work or contribute most of the ideas: therefore, be prepared to defend yourself against the charm and sway of your Taurean friend or loved one.

Taurus is symbolized by the placid bull, the male of the bovine animal. The bull derives from a wild species but has been domesticated since recorded history as an agent in the reproduction of either milk cows or draw oxen.

The bull may graze and remain docile for a very long period of time; but when angered, he may rush or stampede, leading the herd to follow in the onslaught. Herds are led by a bull who has proven his superiority by fighting against all who would contest his position, but those fighting matches are seldom fatal. Their strong protective natures guard the cows and calves from any sort of outside danger. When preparing to attack, their heads bend low as they snort and paw the ground.

The bull's gentle, enticing manner is evident in the face. These bovine features are exaggerated in some who possess a large bone structure, but the bovine appearance will always stand out somewhat, regardless.

The bull has large, flared nostrils that may wiggle when he displays any kind of emotion. When making decisions, the bull audibly snorts or pants or sighs as if he is fatigued. Bulls love to smell home cooking, perfume, pine needles, or freshly mown hay and have an acute memory of odors.

The chin always stands out from a fine little round ball to a large protruding bulb. The jawbone is often square and prominent. Guys sometimes emphasize their chins by wearing beards or goatees.

The bull has soft, round alluring eyes that are enhanced by long, curvy lashes. When the bull is satisfied he blinks slowly, fluttering those lashy lids up and down like the signalman's box on the deck of a destroyer.

There's nothing else quite like the warm, silent approval of a Taurean blink. The whole face moves upward as the eyes close. He also winks often, especially when he is giving his approval. The wink is accompanied by a smile, of course. On some, the eyes are not so big and round but have an exaggerated slant either downward, looking sad and forelorn, or upward, looking almond shaped.

Like most other features on the bull's face, his eyebrows are soft and curvy, containing an abundance of curly hairs, which the bull often trims to improve neatness. Eyebrows aren't likely to curve or arch but to fill out the full allotment of the space provided for them. There is a thick fleshy area underneath the outer ends of the eyebrows.

The mouth is full and sensuous. Lips appear succulent and kissable. In fact, those Taurean lips often pucker in gestures of silent approval or disapproval or speak words that will command. Taureans are authoritative, but they show authority ever so nicely so that it doesn't hurt so much when they criticize. Taureans lick their lips often, moving the tongue back and forth or in and out the way cows do when they graze.

You will find a wide forehead adorning the Taurean face and an absence of a widow's peak on the hairline, which is a Scorpionic feature: the Taurean polarity. I often see acne scars on Taurus-rising people. I think this is attributable to their delicate skin, which is easily irritated - a figurative as well as literal condition.

White bulls usually have curly hair. If someone tells me that he has Taurus rising and the hair is as straight as a string, I assume the birth time is off. Not only is the hair curly but also there's a lock of hair that persists in dropping across the forehead into the eyes. If you let your imagination run just a little, you will see the bull's horn in that lock that refuses to stay back with the rest of the hair. Your Taurean subject takes extra care in his appearance: beauty runs from head-tip to tip-toe.

The bull speaks with a tone of authority, even though his voice is sometimes soft and melodious. Guys usually have deep voices; gals have soft, warm ones. Although your bull may be dead wrong, he probably sounds as if he knows exactly what he's talking about. There's no one who can reassure you as well as can Ferdinand.

The body shape is usually stocky and solid, especially on guys. Bulls carry extra weight in their shoulders and also in their chests.

The neck may appear short because he holds his shoulders high as if to sport a constant shrug. Gals are not so inclined to carry shoulders high but are inclined to emphasize their upper arms in most gestures and movements. Regardless of the body weight or size, the body emphasis is in the torso. Legs seem short by comparison and seldom carry extra pounds even when the bull is overweight. Extra pounds are carried in the abdomen, and guys seem to carry it all the way up through their chests to the tops of their necks. Upper arms will easily expand with overweight whether the bull is fat or thin, but his lower arms and legs taper off toward rather small hands and feet.

The bull walks with a solid step, feet applied softly yet firmly and with deliberation. Don't worry about inviting this bull to your china shop for Taurus-rising people are not clumsy and may even be exceptionally graceful. They make good dancers but prefer traditional dances over the latest steps.

Your first glance will show you the gentle, patient person who usually takes over when there's nobody left to fix the problem. Although deliberate, Taurus will commit himself to people and things in order to get the job done, even though he isn't likely to pitch in until the "eleventh hour." They are thorough, however, and set their own paces. If you are waiting for your bull to finish up a job for you, be careful not to distract, to rush, or to interrupt him.

Of all the signs, Taurus is the most attractive when overweight. This, too, has its limits; but those full features lend themselves to a full body. Like the natives of the other Venus-ruled sign, Libra, the Taurean is often on a diet; and like the sign of the scales, the bull is also a meal skipper.

Unlike a Libran, however, a Taurean enjoys a hearty meal of meat and potatoes and plenty of bread and gravy, too. The bull enjoys grazing on salad greens and can lose his head over pies, cakes, and other scrumptuous baked goods. He enjoys plenty of medium-rare roast beef and eats it leisurely as he sips good wine. He also enjoys lapping up huge tankards of ale and knows all the best restaurants in town.

Bulls are fond of soft pastels and flowery prints. Harsh colors and poor color combinations can enrage the bull as does a red cape used on el Toro in the bullring. Guys prefer blue-grays and beiges or warm tones but not dark colors. All Taureans are fond of leather clothing and all fabric with a texture that feels sumptuous.

Guys expect their gals to look feminine and alluring. They prefer their women in skirts and long dresses over slacks and jeans. They rarely throw anything away and can dress up that fifteen-year-old frock or suit to make it look like the peak of fashion. The cloth is always of good quality, even if the style doesn't catch your eye. Bulls enjoy chokers and all chains and ornaments worn high on the chest or around the neck.

Activity often centers around the table. There's nothing better to the bull's sense of well being than to involve himself in family get-togethers when all the matrons bring their prized dishes. When the bull isn't fondering around the festive board, he is probably relaxing in the afternoon shade or observing something pretty and pleasant. Taureans are natural gardeners and seem to have a built-in taste for fine art. In fact, many are artists themselves.

Mental contests are preferred to active ones, but bulls excel in games that allow them to annihilate their opponents. Although he's a bit slow on the uptake, one should step out of the bull's way whenever he is running towards him. Bulls don't stop for any reason before they reach their marks. They are usually fond of bowling, hockey and football. Gals favor sports that won't detract from their lady-like appearances; therefore, a lot depends on the current social standards in women's sports and activities.

Taureans look for marriage partners who are steady and loyal and who will be willing to sacrifice a measure of their own success for that of the bull's. He may ask the partner to deny himself material comforts as well, feeling that this denial demonstrates some measure of the partner's dedication and love. In fact, a Taurean may try to keep his mate wholly to himself, so possessive is he on occasion. He can drive a loved one away by smothering him with too much love and attention.

Taureans seek community favor by giving their hearts and time in projects and charities. They contribute their time and concern for youth, often patting themselves on the back with each good deed. They strive to behave and dress in the latest fashion but sometimes pull it off badly, for they are conservative.

The bull demands loyalty and devotion from everyone within his circle, by shouting, stomping, pleading, and crying for total devotion. Taurean security needs go deep into the centers of the hearts and do not stop short of an expectation for one hundred percent commitment from everyone around.

Stubbornness is the bull's most annoying characteristic. He can be rock solid in his decision-making, with or without reason. He sometimes has a "tin-lizzie" morality as codes by which he abides and can be highly critical of the younger generation, especially of his own children.

They don't always understand one's desire for full, individual freedom. They may impose their wills on loved ones to such an extent that the endeared is driven away. Likewise, they can pry too much into another's privacy. Even though your Taurean subject doesn't seem very physically active, it would be unwise to remind him or you may find yourself confronted with an angry bull.

They don't anger easily or often but when they do, watch out! Dishes fly, windows are broken and furniture smashed.

Fortunately, these tempestuous explosions don't occur more than about once yearly (good thing) then your bull is back to his sweet, docile self once again. Your bull also has a tendency to be lazy and a procrastinator of nearly every thing on the agenda. He will get to it in good measure; just don't push! Some bulls don't face their financial responsibilities squarely but borrow or finagle Daddy's money. Sometimes the bull charges most adeptly with his credit card!

A Taurean is placid, however, whose loving-kindness springs from a vulnerable heart. The bull is not an over-achiever, as a rule, but a loyal doer. He sees only one way to do things - - his own way.

He was born to guard and to guide you toward the good life filled with comfort, beauty, and ease. Granted, he seems to take it upon himself to decide from whom and when you need protection and guidance. The bull means no harm; thus, it's up to you to tell him gently that you can manage by yourself.

Getting the point across is another problem! Therefore, gals, if you have a dirty old bull on your hands, love him and enjoy every minute of it because he's yours for life. He's not about to let you trade him in for somebody else. And guys, your Taurean gal is a precious jewel indeed; for you see, she invented the word "lovely."

Fixed   **SCORPIO**   **Water**

ruler: Pluto
(Old ruler, Mars)

Scorpions need to have something precious to cling to. They're almost never light and superficial about anything but approach life with passion and a positive goal in mind. You will find these tenacious creatures wherever there's a challenge that requires an abundance of heart, souls and guts.

Scorpionic guys apply intensity toward getting their jobs done or just about anything else that's important to them. They're shrewd in business, politics, and research; but you can't tell these books by their covers. Their quietness may be mistaken for either shyness or a secretive manner. They're cautious about everyone around them and test others' loyalty before they extend their trust.

Scorpionic gals have an intensity that will either lure or repel you. They totally involve themselves with everything they do and may dedicate themselves to a cause or to a fellow they feel they can't live without. Scorpionic gals make great business people, but the business world isn't their only shining star because they excel in almost anything they undertake and even approach motherhood as if it were a career. Be especially careful of criticizing her children for the original "Jewish Mother" was patterned after the Scorpionic gal.

Scorpio is symbolized by the scorpion; a venomous creature related to the spider. Their curved tails contain poison glands that the scorpion uses in self defense or in occasional attacks launched against an enemy. The females may also attack and devour the males after copulation. The scorpion may sting itself when its very life is threatened, but most scorpions possess a degree of immunity to their own poisons.

Scorpions live most of their lives in isolation except when mating or while the mother cares for her young, which she carries on her back. They are sensitive to slight climate changes and hide underground when the weather is dry. Although the scorpion is a fearsome creature, his will and determination are unequalled in the animal world. A well-fed scorpion can survive for several months without food or water.

Scorpions were meant to entice and to endure: two abilities that seem contradictory to each other; yet, these abilities create the basis for the Scorpionic gaze which is intense and unforgettable. No matter their color, those eyes seem to be direct descendants of the laser beam. Although it may not literally burn holes through your vest, that gaze will surely etch a place in your memory.

It's sometimes easy to confuse the shape of the eyes with that of the bull's. The eyes of all races often have a wide space between them. On many, the eyes curve downward at the outer corners, but other Scorpionic eyes slant upward and are almond shaped.

Regardless of the slant, the eyes are usually full, round, and heavily lashed. The scorpion is likely to stare at you intently as you talk to him, oblivious to the activity anywhere else in the surrounding area. He seldom forgets anything he's ever seen and has a ready file of scenes within his memory bank that he's photographed with his mental camera.

The Scorpionic nose may be shaped in a hook with a prominent curve from the middle of the nose bridge to the tip. The hooked nose on Scorpio-rising people has often been misunderstood as an eagle's beak. As I mention in the Introduction, I consider the eagle as representative of Aquarius, not Scorpio. I think the confusion started when someone misunderstood the eagle for the phoenix, a mythical bird easily associated with Scorpio, as he is known to rise from the ashes of defeat, rising vertically toward new heights of greatness. Noses on some other scorpions take on the classical soft, rounded appearance found also in many Cancerian and Piscean people.

Eyebrows are often thick and bushy but not always. When the brows are trimmed, they are done so in a dramatic way. Slender, dramatic eyebrows usually started out as thick, bushy ones, anyway.

The Scorpion's lips are full and succulent. The Scorpion shares with his Taurean polarity a love of good food, wine, and the taste of one with whom he is passionately involved. While either the Taurean or the Scorpion seems eager to taste and to kiss, the Scorpion considers self-denial a virtue and may avoid self-indulgence with anything or anyone he is tempted toward. The more he wants it, the more likely he will be to do without it. Of all the signs, Scorpio is the most strong-willed; and the Scorpion takes pride in his own abstinence.

Teeth glisten as the alluring scorpion smiles. Yet, I can't say whether it's the teeth themselves or the message behind the smile that seems so magnetic. Maybe you can tell me when you've been struck by it yourself. Incidentally, Scorpionic teeth can be mistaken for the flash of a Gemini smile; but the Scorpion smiles far less often that does the Geminian.

The promiment jawbone is an outstanding clue in Scorpionic features. It's big and square and is sometimes used to express emotion, appearing strong enough to crunch steel or bones; thus, you'd be best off to assume a running position should you ever insult or offend a scorpion. In his solitary life

style, the scorpion sets his jaw in a display of determination that leaves little doubt that he is clearly capable of finishing the job he's set out to do.

The hair encircles the face rather closely, or is combed down and around, nearly touching and sometimes coverning, part of the eyes. Although the hair style may not be memorable, the glisten may attract your attention. A widow's peak may stand out on the forehead if the hair is combed back.

Scorpions speak quietly but with a tone of command in their voices so that everyone else in the room will either speak more softly or stop talking altogether when the scorpion speaks up. They talk a lot about themselves and especially about their children. Scorpions choose words carefully and are not inclined to make grammatical mistakes. They often learn correct grammar and pronounciation by listening to the radio and by emulating those they respect.

The Scorpionic body shape is usually compact and solid. Although they are often a little smaller in size than are the other signs, they seem larger. On the other hand, there's a

Scorpionic body shape that's spider-like - - all arms and legs. Either the body shape is small and compact or long and leggy.

Whichever the body type, there is a muscle tension that is always evident, creating a need within the scorpion's life style to exercize extensively as a means of relaxation. Although the muscles are prominent, they are attractive unless excess weight hides the basic body structure. Generally, the tendency is toward slightness all over with an emphasis on strength. Remember that the scorpion relies on her own physical strength and endurance to make it through the arid summers or to support her young, which she carries with her on her back.

Scorpions walk softly with a gently slide of the foot both as it touches the ground and lifts up on the return. Scorpions tip-toe with ease and do so whether or not they're eavesdropping. They watch where they're going and walk most surely in soft and muddy or marshy places where danger lurks underfoot.

Your first glance will show you the determined creature who views life as a constant challenge to be met and conquered. The firm jaw, the muscle tension, and the intense gaze and manner are all special to the magnetic scorpion who lures his prey into his path and then claims it as his own personal property.

Likewise, respect and dedication toward other people and other causes make the scorpion stand out in any crowd. No one can serve or lead better than can the scorpion, and both qualities are equal within the same person.

A scorpion eats and drinks as if each morsel and swallow of food and drink were sacraments in the worship of his health and well being. But when the scorpion is disappointed or discouraged with himself, he may turn on himself with an eating or drinking binge that can last for weeks or months. Eventually, the overindulgence will take its toll. Only then is this tenacious person capable of enduring the long and bitter task of self-denial, restoring his weight and health to normal once again.

The scorpion may sting himself when he feels endangered. Likewise, the Scorpionic person may willingly allow surgery to remove important body parts whenever he is disappointed or angry with himself. Other chronic and debilitating illnesses are sometimes tolerated as measures of atonement and self-inflicted punishment whenever the Scorpion views his past actions as less than admirable and worthy. It is wise for all Scorpions to learn the lessons of forgiveness, especially to the self.

A Scorpion identifies himself with his clothing. His clothes speak of the group he is trying to lure into his inner circle. Dark, conservative clothes show he's appealing to the business world or the clergy; bangles and beads, the Youth Cult, and sporty apparel speaks of an identity with the suburban station-wagon crowd. However your Scorpion dresses, you're sure to spot something

about him that attracts your eye, making it hard to concentrate while you're looking at him. Scorpionic women sometimes wear earrings that dangle and glitter like fish lures. And should she decide to go after that big fish, she can deck herself out in the most alluring outfit designed to destroy any trace of competition. She knows her strength and allure; therefore, she's careful in selecting the clothes she wears.

Sports provide a natural arena to the scorpion. In each contest, the scorpion intends to prove his natural superiority. He enjoys strenuous, and sometimes death-defying sports geared totally to conquer the enemy - - or the contestant. He's a dreadful loser and would rather die than take second place. They're natural business people, excelling when the going gets the roughest. They enjoy politics for the life/death contest it offers.

At night, Scorpions can be seen prowling the streets, dropping into coffee shops, nightclubs, and all-night grocery stores; but many Scorpions fear the night and lock themselves tightly inside their homes to curl up by the telephone or to watch television until the test pattern comes on. Many are natural psychics and may spend their time "reading" for others, although they seldom like to "read" for anyone but themselves. They enjoy mystery stories and have a tendency to dwell on death.

Scorpions enjoy marriage for the emotional security it provides them. They select a partner who is tolerant and patient with their extremism, their fears and their obsessions. They are best suited to someone in whom they have complete trust: a loved one who will understand their needs, even though they may never whisper of their anxieties or their discontent. Partners must be committed to a lifetime relationship, for the Scorpion doesn't eliminate a mate who is still on his feet and breathing. And lest you forget, to betray a Scorpion is to sign a death warrant on yourself. All the excuses in the world won't make up for the mistakes you've made unless, of course, your Scorpionic mate knows he had it coming, in which case he may be willing to wipe the slate clean and to begin again. He may never mention the incident again; but he will never, never forget it.

Security needs are met through companionship with many different types of people. especially with those who are intelligent and idealistic. A Scorpion is most liberal with his own family, ironically, but doesn't always take kindly to Bohemian behavior from others in his midst. Ultimate goals are sought through a vision that someday he will be in full charge - - noticed and recognized as a leader who will be remembered long after he is gone.

Suspicion and bitterness are the Scorpion's most annoying characteristics. He can be vindictive, cunning, cruel, and just downright mean in nearly every category. He can hold a grudge for years and hang onto a worthless mate or become involved with undesirable people just to prove a negative point.

They are natural satirists, whose piercing words are capable of peeling the paint off metal; but they're by far the most sincere and dedicated people in all the world. If they believe in you, they will give themselves completely, no holds barred.

He was born to dedicate himself totally to you. He's yours for the keeping as long as you demonstrate your sincerity and your honorable intentions; that is, if he'll have you. He is a harsh judge of character; but if you're worthy of his admiration and respect, he will follow you to the ends of the earth, and then some.

Fixed   **LEO**   **Fire**

ruler:the Sun

A Leonian has to be the center of attention. In order to supply him with the quantity of loyalty and devotion the lion requires, everyone within his circle has to bow just a little. But that royal magnificence will make your acts of humility worth the trouble, and you will share pride with the rest of his kingdom in knowing and loving your most regal Leonian friend or loved one.

A Leonian guy is especially strong willed, and capable of taking charge of nearly all situations. He commands and orders in such a natural way that you couldn't possibly think of refusing his requests. He lives to love and loves to live. He EXPECTS to be waited on; to be calmed and caressed from the sweat and rigors of his most recent conquest.

Leonian gals are born queens. They may measure the limits of their empires at the backyard fence, for their subjects are the most important people in her world; they are her husband and the heirs to the throne of her own private empire. (Just in case your Leonian doesn't happen to have a spouse and cubs, he has substitutes for both. Substitutes can be found in the classroom, at the office, or throughout the neighborhood.)

Leonians are magnanimous and magnificent in their personal encounters. Each expects to live in opulence, and each demands nothing less than total devotion and loyalty from everyone on whom he depends.

Leo is symbolized by the lion, King of the Jungle. The lion is a large, powerfully built cat with a long body, short legs, and well-developed muscles. His most outstanding feature is his full, hairy mane, which surrounds his face and continues down the shoulders, throat, and chest.

A lion's territory is clearly marked by his grunts and growls, but territorial boundary lines change almost daily according to the available food supply. Lions live together in prides of a dozen or more with several lionesses and partly grown cubs. Lions hunt by night and sleep by day.

The Leonian was born to love and be loved. He considers it his birthright to take charge over other people. He is naturally fierce and courageous but soft and tender. Leonians express their love with those big, soft, round pussy-cat eyes. Other Leonian eyes are almond shaped, slanting upward at the outer corners.

The allure of the eyes is a special trademark and can be spotted on nearly all lions, regardless of racial backgound. The eyes are playful and seem to hold on to their youth and innocence far beyond the limits of youth and innocence. In fact, lions don't ever give up their innocence entirely but clutch it to their larger-than-life hearts until that last fading purr.

Innocence shows, too, in the eyes, and should never be considered any sort of deceit of treachery. You can be sure that if a lion is thinking deceit; it, too, will show. Because the Leonian is the child who is never willing to accept the responsibilities of maturity at the cost of his childish joy, a child-like naivete will persist throughout his life.

Leonian faces seem more complete. His lashes are longer, curlier, and fuller. Lips are full, round, and expressive, revealing each mood as it takes place in the lion's heart. Leonian smiles are totally beguiling.

Many white Leonians have long, straight noses. These Leonians with prominent, aquiline noses have the ability to get what they want by demanding it. They challenge everything as they go along, sometimes for the self-satisfaction of giving orders. They seldom lose in a contest.

Many other Leonians have pussy-cat noses that are notice- ably small. Small-nosed Leonians are generally less demanding, but it takes more than a nose to judge these cats.

The lion's mane is another special Leonian trademark. It's unusual to find a short-haired lion. As a rule, their hair is long and combed or piled high in eye-catching appeal. When emotions run high or, when the lion's turned on by somebody, he will caress his hair, purring softly all the while.

On the other hand, when pressure mounts and emotions run high in the lion's life, he will roar and growl while he flips his own hair around, or will quickly pass his hands through it in gestures of torment. A lioness may throw her head backward or sideways dramatically as she flips that gorgeous mane from her shoulders. Even short-haired lions touch their hair often and use it in their own special ways to display their emotions. They twist curls, caress waves, and comb through it  as if to comb away the hassles they're encountering at the time.

Leonian guys are fond of facial hair, especially moustaches, which they frequently twist and caress. Although gals aren't able to grow those whiskers, they may touch and caress their cheeks, eyebrows, and necks just as cats primp and preen.

The lion's voice is playful, commanding, pleading, piercing, whispery, and soulful. All these tones and inflections are displayed in a remarkably short span of time, especially when the lion is trying to win points at salesmanship or romance. The voice is the voice of an actor or actress, for he is as natural off the stage as he is on it.

Leonian bodies usually emphasize the shoulders and torso. The lion needs a large chest to inflate when he is filled with pride and a big cavity to hold that larger-than-life heart. His legs will be a little shorter than average but beautifully muscled. The hips will be slimmer but the shoulders wider. The buttocks, for their diminuitive size, are round, firm, and build for running and prancing. Gals often have small bustlines, although it won't look like it at first glance because of their beautiful posture. Excellent posture is a Leonian trademark of either sex.

Lions walk with graceful steps that involve their entire bodies. They tip-toe a few steps at a time and then step firmly, able to turn or step sideways with little effort. They can leap across a room (or stage) like chorus-line girls or guys or stomp-stomp around the house like little kids having a temper tantrum. As in most other gestures and movements of the lion, his step and walk will express his emotion; and you will have a good idea of his mood before he even comes in the front door.

Your first glance will help you determine whether you're looking at the King or Queen of Beasts or at one of his jungle subjects from the other eleven signs. His slightly tipped head will be held high above in a proud stance. His manners and come-hither arrogance will stand out as obvious clues. Should he feel any sort of defeat or discouragement, however, you should be aware that everyone within his circle will know of the dilemma. They enjoy sharing all things; and in their sharing, they expect their loyal subjects to help solve their problems either with or for them.

Lions enjoy eating rare meat and just about anything and everything that goes with it. They enjoy fare fit for a king and queen, eating heartily while gathering regal companions about them as they partake of the festive board. Sumptuous dinners surrounded by lots of activity and noise make lions purr and roar with laughter.

They would rather be hosts than guests and are generous to a fault, demanding that you bring the children along to a dinner. As a guest, don't be dismayed at the dogs and children running around the dining area. Even Virgoan ascendants will gradually fall into the raucous activity, feeling as you leave that that special dinner party was one of your fondest memories. Dieting is so painful to Leo that it is usually achieved only through religious pennance or a sojourn to a retreat.

Leonians wear clothes made of rich, sumptuous fabric. The styles may sometimes be a bit out of date, but the decorative trim and elaborate jewelry will more than make up for it. Guys go for silk ties and velvets, and gals love to dress up in long skirts and furs.

Big rings, showy medallions and other elaborate jewelry add both weight and worth to the Leonian wardrobe - - all in gold, of course. Clothing is colorful, in rich hues, sometimes to the extreme of poor taste, but always worn with flair. Lions wear black in mourning only.

Lions enjoy contests that display all of their physical skills. Although they don't like to lose, Leonians take pride in losing to those whose skill and prowess are superior to their own. They've enjoyed the match; and after the contest, each player and all the spectators must gather 'round the table for huge tankards of ale. Even when a loser, the lion will brag about his own part of the match. Later on, the lion will brag even more about the stout and brave competitor who left him in the rubble of defeat.

Lions are generally more physical than mental, but they enjoy games of strategy played indoors when the weather is too cold for spectators to watch from the stands. Cold winter days (and nights) are more likely spent rehearsing for a play or in the pursuit of a lover to play a companion role on his own private stage.

The Leonian is fond of children and gives his time and money generously to all the cubs of the world. He is especially proud of his own offspring and genuine about all the affection he showers on them. The lion wants his own cubs to be "chips off the old block" and expects them to follow directly in his own footsteps.

When the children decide to go their own ways upon graduation from high school, the Leonian may roar in wounded, anguished wails that he has failed as a parent or that kids don't respect their parents any more. Lions must learn to respect their children's freedom of choice as much as they respect the freedom of others. Leo is deeply religious and gives generously of his time and his money to the church or the temple.

Lions look for one who will be at least mentally equal or perhaps even superior to them in marriage and partnership. Even in business partnerships, lions expect the partner to do much of their thinking for them (and most of the work).

Marriage is a very special institution that may be entered into when there is a strong possibility of an heir to the throne. Leonian guys often believe in that old saw, "keep your gal pregnant in Summer and barefoot in Winter." Marriage also provides the means by which the king or queen establishes his own kingdom. Loved ones must be loyal above all other human qualities - - devoted, honorable, and true. An Eagle Scout would be a perfect mate.

Security needs are met through repeated tests of loyalty from those within the lion's inner circle. His pride is easily wounded, consequently, he feels most secure around friends and loved ones. Leonians are often uncomfortable among strangers.

Goals most coveted to the Leonian's breast lie in the attainment of a large bank account and lots of material goods that appear to prove to everyone that he is truly worth his weight in gold. He dreams that someday he will own a large estate complete with servants and a luxuriant green lawn set aside for occasional games of croquet.

Arrogance is the lion's most annoying characteristic. He intensely dislikes taking orders but will do so from one he considers more intelligent or experienced than he. He brags about nearly everything he has even done and doesn't understand why everyone isn't speelbound by it. He often thinks his is the most devastating problem in the world at the time and sometimes lends very little support to others who are in the same dilemmas at other times. He is sometimes loud, boisterous, and demanding - - embarrassing loved ones and offending strangers as he roars commands to everyone around him.

Leonians expect to be waited on and dislike menial chores like housework and trivial paper pushing. Some are lazy, expecting their families to do their share of the work while they loaf. This is true of gals and guys alike, not to mention

indolent cubs. Some prefer to sleep by day and to dance by night, prowling old haunts for familiar faces and new adventures.

Although they expect unfaultering loyalty from their loved ones, they don't always play by the same rules. Leonian guys are notorious romancing Romeos, but Leonian gals are more inclined to be true to one man. Even if he's a wanderer, he will keep one special gal in his heart who will be there for life. You see, he's loyal after all but in his own way.

Despite all the lion's faults, he is seldom petty or insensitive. He simply can't bear to think that there is anyone out there in the world who considers him calloused, stingy, or dishonest.

He was born to rule and to shower the world with love and affection as only lions know how to do so well. His heart is sometimes bigger than his brains, but his respect for everyone else grows with each response from friends and loved ones, and from admiring strangers as well. A lion won't ask you to change. He will love you with all the depth and innocence of a child; for, you see, the Leonian will always remain a child in his heart.

Fixed AQUARIUS Air

ruler: Uranus

(old ruler, Saturn)

An Aquarian needs to be involved with everybody in the whole world. When he isn't involved, he needs aloneness in order to keep that electric battery cell of his humming. Although you can't tell by the name, Aquarius is an air sign, not a water sign. The stuff the water bearer is pouring from his urn isn't droplets at all but electrical currents. Still other astrologers consider the urn's contents to be ethers of knowledge, a symbol of one of the Aquarian's main tasks - - the distribution of knowledge.

An Aquarian guy is tolerant toward all people regardless of their stations in life. He disregards their national origins and their creeds and colors and is especially equality-minded toward women. An Aquarian gal is tolerant, too, and is less inclined to submit to the traditional feminine role than are her sisters in the other eleven signs.

Both guys and gals are dedicated toward socially balanced values. Each recognizes his responsibility in bringing about the changes. Today's cultural values are nearly intolerable in their outmoded concepts; tomorrow's values are all that matter in the Aquarian's search to find his place in life.

Therefore, if you think all that social involvement can make the Aquarian serious and often worrisome, you're right. Your Aquarian friend or loved one carries more than his share of social burdens on his back.

Aquarius is symbolized by the water bearer, the youth whose task is to provide all working men and women a cool drink from his urn as they toil in the fields or in other tasks. He shares the water from his urn with everyone regardless of each one's station in life. In many ways, the water bearer has been chosen by society to carry the burdens of his community while others scrap for superior positions.

In keeping with the animal symbols of most of the zodiac, I would like to substitute the eagle for the water bearer as a symbol of the sign. The eagle is a proud and majestic bird whose task appears to carry the burden of wild animal extinction for his fellow animals.

He bothers few on this planet; yet, he has been singled out as a target for merciless hunters. His intelligence (symbol of the Aquarian as well) inspires him to maintain the same mate for life and to return to the same nest each year in order that the pair may hatch their young. He is a symbol of democracy and of greatness, of reaching upward above the riff-raff of life toward to perfection of body, soul and spirit.

The Aquarian features speak of friendliness, concern, and a desire to share all he has with his fellow man. Therefore, these qualities are clearly evident in the facial features and throughout the entire body as well. His smile is genuine, and his eyes are warm and friendly. His eyes sparkle and dance; yet, they seem to remain detached from any sort of close personal involvement with you or with anyone else.

From time to time, that sparkle is replaced with flashes of intense curiosity and a total involvment with either something he is saying or trying to hear. The Aquarian seems to have a radar receiver for picking up on conversations from great distances. And alas, there will be many times when your Aquarian ins't listening at all but is rather computing your manner of speech, your mood, and the knowledge he has already filed away about you. He has an eagle eye for spotting trouble both nearby and far away or far ahead, but it's doubtful that your eagle will pass his observations on to you.

Most Aquarian features are difficult to describe from a physical point of view, for they are varied and diverse. The Uranian rulership of the sign creates a strong tendency for Aquarius-rising people to look like their Sun signs. Don't forget that Uranus is the planetary indicator of reversals.

The Aquarian smile is broad and genuine and filled with concern for whoever happens to be close by. He shares his smiles and his friendly manner as easily with a stranger as with a beloved friend. Your Aquarian may smile only once in a while if he's the worrisome type who carries the world on his shoulders.

Many Aquarians have oval shaped faces, but others have only an oval forehead. (Should your Aquarian resemble his Sun sign or the sign in which the ruler of his ascendant is placed, these rules will not apply.) Aquarian cheekbones are seldom prominent, a differing feature from the previous sign Capricorn, which is exclusively Saturn ruled. Saturn's old rulership over Aquarius may be evident in facial lines, however. Many eagles possess less facial hair than do their brothers of the other eleven signs.

I have always heard that people with Aquarius rising put streaks in their hair or wear it in a shocking manner that runs against the grain of the Establishment. Although it's true that some Aquarians are pace-setters, most others are preoccupied in identifying with a group and feel conspicuous standing out solitarily. Without meaning to, sometimes the Aquarian looks as if he's just pulled his finger out of an electric socket; and his hair stands out in wild disarray to prove it. Some male eagles tend toward baldness in early adulthood.

The voice is either soft, slow, and gentle or harsh as an eagle's screech with a cackle to match. You probably won't find both characteristics within the same person, for the Aquarian is consistent in his means of expression.

The Aquarian body shape seems to be designed to accomodate the life style of the coming space age. Although their height is a little greater than the average height of today's man and woman, the muscle tone is less, thus creating a slender appearance. When this is not the case, the muscles will be obviously prominent, reminding one of Saturn's old rulership. The Aquarian body is not designed to do much physical work or to carry any excess weight.

When extra pounds find their way to the Aquarian male or female body, they are almost always carried in the most uncomfortable places where they will show the most. Guys sometimes develop wide hips and gals fill out in the shoulders! Veins are prominent in both arms and legs, and Aquarians often complain of circulation problems.

Noise bothers Aquarians; hence, they prefer shoes that don't squeek or click – probably sneakers. In fact, I have seen a significant number of them walking on their tip-toes even when running. They seem to be practicing up for a running start for the big take off they will make some day. Eagles walk lightly; they were born to fly.

As you gaze at the Aquarian male or female, you will see a soul who is torn between remaining here on earth to help mankind yet who feels a passionate urge to fly beyond the clouds. He is committed to fulfilling his destiny and will remain within the mainstream out of a sense of obligation. He looks hard into the future; but should he disclose his futuristic thoughts to you, he will only do so because he thinks you to be wise enough to understand what he is saying. He cares little whether or not you agree with him.

Aquarians should eat as though they were tightly nestled inside a space capsule. Now what is there to eat on the ENTERPRISE? - - you've got it - - lots of condensed food and vitamin pills. The Child of the Universe is not built to digest today's heavy food and must be especially careful to avoid junk food. His mission flight to Mercury can best be made on a body nourished by fruits and vegetables. In fact, an Aquarian often prefers to be a vegetarian and would be happiest if he could somehow gather nourishment from the air.

Water bearers dress according to the dictates of the group with which they identify. Although it's true that gals don't like to dress in the conventional feminine dress and guys don't care for suits and ties, they will dress in the manner that will enable them to swing the most votes toward their idealistic causes. They feel best when dressed in shocking pure white regardless of the fabric or style and prefer clothes that lack frills, trims, or buckles.

Sports and activities are nearly always centered around intellectual endeavors unless the chart shows a strong tendency otherwise. Because of the Aquarian's serious nature, he may find work his only outlet. This is especially true when others are leaning on him for a result, as in a laboratory experiment.

Aquarians are not noted as good business people, for they  are too generous and sometimes naive when they are told a sad story.

They enjoy making crafts and are highly inventive, imaginative, and creative. They like to commune with nature and may give up a successful career at its height if they are not able to realize the inner peace so vital to their senses of well being. Although the eagle may work hard for you with his mind, he won't use his muscles unless he doesn't see any way out of it. He enjoys all social involvements and is often found in clubs and organizations or in political activities.

Aquarians marry people they like, not those they love. They are fearful of forming close, dependent relationships and find it difficult to do so. Yet the Child of the Universe seeks out a lifetime mate who will demonstrate an abundance of love and devotion toward him.

Security needs come, oddly enough, from a set income, a steady job, and a permanent home with trees and garden space. If he's going to commit himself to this planet, the Aquarian might just as well make the most of it. His ultimate goal is his desire to leave a mark on the universe through his creative works, words, and deeds that will remain and endure long after he has gone.

Aquarians' most annoying characteristics center around their opinionated viewpoints. They are dogmatic about most issues and highly critical toward others who do not agree with them. In fact, they have plenty of opinions on matters with which they are familiar, as well as on those topics about which they know little, if anything. They have opinions on political and not-to-well-known figures, prices where to buy what, and everything else on earth and in the universe. To say that the Aquarian is a know-it-all is to put it mildly.

Aquarians abhor stupidity almost as much as they abhor outmoded prejudices and unthought-out attitudes and opinions. They are intellectual to a fault and can sometimes be accused of "living in their heads." In other words, they do not react on emotional impulse but only through their thinking processes.

Don't bother asking them for an opinion unless you really want one. You will surely receive a long speech on aesthetic values, historical background, cultural and community usefulness, and the potential for the future. They may not barrage you with big words, but they will probably throw a lot of technical words your way, especially words that have a psychological basis to them. They seldom involve themselves seriously in religious practice, and many are professed atheists.

Aquarians can see ahead into the far distant future, but they often have trouble looking ahead to see what will happen next week. They won't lie about the mistakes they've made and are often open and honest in disclosing their own foolishness to anyone whose knowledge they respect. When they've accomplished something great and illuminating, they will share the laurels with everyone else involved in the project.

They can, however, become a jangled heap of nerve ends or can fly off in a dozen directions with little purpose in mind. Don't make a lot of noise, ask stupid questions, or loaf while the group is working; that is, unless you want the water bearer to pull the plug in his urn and dump cold water on top of your head! Their warmth may surprise you as may their coolness, for they are personal about impersonal matters and impersonal about personal ones.

Just when you've had enough -- when you're ready to cry "uncle" – your Aquarian foe will turn out to be the best friend you've ever had. He will help you when you're down and will seldom criticize or belabor a point if you are really in a mess; nor will he spread your follies to your mutual associates, for he truly understands human failing and is not inclined to judge individual mistakes. You probably won't realize these virtues of your Aquarian friend or loved one until the chips are down, however; therefore, don't remove his name from your Christmas card list.

Aquarians were born to befriend you and to lead you out of the darkness of ignorance toward the light of knowledge. True love doesn't bind but rather liberates its loved ones to realize their total capabilities. Your Aquarian loved one will guide you and will share with you in the most enduring love known to mankind, for your Aquarian will love you as a friend.

The MUTABLE SIGNS:

Gemini

Sagittarius

Virgo

Pisces

Mutable   **GEMINI**   **Air**

ruler: Mercury

A Geminian has to know the reasons for everything. In fact, his favorite word is "why." You will find these curious people wherever they can poke their noses into places and things in order to meet the largest number of people and to try to learn what makes them tick. As a matter of fact, they're curious about nearly everything in life and ferret out information everywhere they can.

Geminian guys are witty, clever, and charming. They can be blunt and cunning or shy and reticent and all in the space of five minutes. All they're trying to do is to get a reaction, to find out something, or to pass the word along. Guys play at winning over the opposite sex as a pastime with seemingly little anxiety involved in their efforts. Even when we know better, most of us gals can easily fall under the spell of a Geminian string of gush and charm. Watch out, gals!

Geminian gals are charming, witty and clever, too – capable of the same curiosity as their male "twins." Both guys and gals keep the action going with their words and movements. No group of people is complete without at least one Gemini-rising person. They're intelligent (at least they seem more witty, worldly and wordy than do the rest of us) and enjoy passing on their most recently acquired information to anyone who has a minute to hear them out.

Gemini is symbolized by the twins -- significant as representatives of the sign by their duality. Because of the humanness of the twins I would like to substitute the swallow as Gemini's symbol, in keeping with the animals of the zodiac.

The swallow is a small, graceful bird. In flight, they move with such deft and speed that few predators can keep up, let alone overtake them. Swallows migrate in flocks, stopping at familiar roosts and returning to their original homes the following season.

Poking their long beaks in and out, bobbing their heads while listening to every sound in their surrounding, the swallow keeps his head in nearly constant motion. Although these precocious birds aren't recognized as song birds, they are quite noisy, setting up an ear-shattering din when roosting at sunset.

Geminians are built to find out about people and things and to pass the news along. Geminians are nosey people; thus, their noses are often their most outstanding characteristic. Like that of a bird, a Geminian's beak is sometimes long and straight and narrow with elongated nostrils. In other cases, the nose takes on the characteristics of the sign in which Gemini's ruler, Mercury, is placed. Blacks won't be able to depend on the Geminian beak most of the time; however, they can depend on the darting eyes, the bobbing head, and the smile -- why, they invented it!

The Geminian smile is his special trademark. The teeth are often oversized, yet straight and even. A pleasant remark, a gesture of approval or just a glance at a friendly face will trigger a twinkle in the eye that is followed a split second later by a grin as broad as and brighter than all the lights in Time's Square.

It seems to me sometimes that Geminian teeth are made that way so that they can bite off all the bits and pieces of information they're always chomping at. Sometimes the twins bite off more than they can chew, despite those oversized teeth. It's easy to make a promise, but it is something else to deliver the goods. Geminian lips are thin on those who listen more than they talk (a rare bird) and thick on those who enjoy savoring their words.

The eyes on the twins are not their most outstanding feature. They are especially warm and friendly, however. But physically, those eyes won't catch your own. That special sparkle may confuse you with the horse's gleam sometimes because of the polarity of Sagittarius. For the most part, the twins' eyes move about with such speed one might think he actually has eyes in the back of his head. He isn't about to miss a single thing going on around him and seems to be able to listen to two conversations at once.

Sometimes the chin takes on the pointedness from the polarity of Sagittarius. Otherwise, the chin is not an out-standing physical feature.

Twins wear their hair in the latest fashion, always with ease of care in mind. Short cuts are most popular on gals, short enough to allow them the freedom to swim during late afternoons, to dance in the evening, and to brush through it early the next morning in time for work. It's unusual to see a head of Geminian hair that's not sparkling clean. Swallows comb through their hair frequently and check to make sure that it's neat.

Geminians chirp their words in a light and breathy way when talking. Words tumble in breezy gusts, followed by short gasps for air and then back to another spurt of words, followed by another gasp for air. You may have trouble separating the sentences as you listen.

And while this animated bird is spilling out his thoughts, his hands will wave, point and make gestures that help him describe what he is talking about. Tie his hands behind him and he may have trouble talking. Geminians laugh easily when they talk and may even laugh when things aren't funny – perhaps to express a feeling of nervousness. Because a Geminian identifies with his words so very much, you will find a wide variety of speech pattern apparent. There are no narrow guidelines in determining the Geminian means of verbal communication. The only rule to apply is that Gemini WILL talk.

Twins look tall even when they aren't, unless they're quite a bit overweight. He has longer-than-average arms and legs. His hands take on special emphasis, and your Geminian subject will tap out his rising sign on the tabletop as he drums his fingers. He also loves to doodle and will write on anything that's closeby. He's actually relaxing, but you'll feel certain that he is nervous and uncomfortable.

Twins step lightly with a click and a quick shuffle. If we were to walk on our hands or on all fours, you wouldn't have any doubt about how to pick out a Gemini walk! He's quick on his toes and spins around on one foot with lightening speed.

You'll notice a prominent cranium on the Geminian subject. The forehead protrudes just a little to suggest extra brain room.

The forehead rolls back in a gentle curve toward the hairline, continuing back on bald heads. The hairline may be higher than average, too, so that the rounded cranium stands out even more. You may also notice the Geminian head protruding forward from the rest of the body, especially on twins who live totally in their heads and don't understand their own instincts and emotions.

Twins pick at little bits of this-and-that rather than do they enjoy a full meal at predetermined times of the day. They are seldom voracious eaters, but they add weight from the frequency of snacks. If you want to treat a Geminian to dinner, take him to a smorgasbord that includes everything from soup to nuts. He's sure to try one bite of everything on the table. At dinner parties, he may overeat just to keep his hands busy, especially if he's trying to keep from talking.

Many Geminians are smokers. In the event that they're not, they're sure to extol the sins of tobacco, painting descriptive pictures of what it will do to your lungs if you should light a cigarette in their presence.

Geminians enjoy clothing that allows them the most freedom of movement and ease of care. Special emphasis is placed on accessories and trims such as scarves or ties and hand-bags with matching hats and gloves. They're fussy about color combinations and clever about making sporty duds look dressy. Geminian closets are filled with simple, neat clothes but plenty of them.

Twins enjoy activities that demand the most of their intellectual resources. Of course, games like chess and crossword puzzles take the lead on their lists of pastimes; but mildly active sports and games of chance, like horse racing, rank high, too. It's important that they be one step ahead of the game at all times in their minds. They don't care much whether or not they win, but they can't bear to play with a sore loser.

Twins are often gifted in crafts. Ceramics and leather-work usually come naturally to them, and they can repair almost anything around the house if they allow a little time to figure it out. They enjoy any kind of work or hobby that allows them to create with their hands.

Although they don't necessarily have to go very far from home, Geminians enjoy traveling. They can pick themselves up out of a temporary slump by jumping into the car and taking off for the afternoon. Trips to other countries are great fun, too; and they love to talk about their most recent trip to anywhere, cornering you with slides and photos. More adventurous birds enjoy the swift flight afforded by the motorcycle, the speedboat and the creame-de-la-creame - the racing car.

Geminians enjoy marriage to one who will inspire them. Because they are so often caught up in a mountain of bits and pieces of trivia, they seek out partners who are able to put all those bits together into a usable philosophical lump. There is a strong possibility of two marriages: the first being of a very short term entered into while this bird was off on a migratory flight.

Security needs are met through a life filled with order and solid, steady work habits. They may be sensitive about their humble origins and strive to modify a poor-but-proud image to the rest of the world. In case he wasn't poor in childhood, he may still feel that he was deprived in some basic way. Ultimate goals are met through their belief that what they do is of service to mankind: silent achievement that will live on even after they are gone.

Gossip is the twin's most annoying characteristic. Their love of tid-bits of information makes it almost impossible for them to keep anything to themselves. Their chattering may also get under your skin. They can't help whispering in church, revealing the plot at the climax of a teary movie. or singing loudest at the local tavern. They exaggerate a story in order to entertain anyone who might be listening and are not above dishonesty. They often talk just to hear themselves talk, and their dishonest statements are not always deeply seated in selfish motives: they make innocent statements only to tantalize the listeners.

Although a Geminian learns foreign languages quickly, he may throw them into the barter, too, just to get a reaction from the native. Yes, he is a laugh a minute; but you're going to have trouble getting a serious, honest remark out of him.

Depending on your Geminian can be a worry. Because talking is such an easy thing for him to do, he answers nearly everything with a "yes," promising the Moon and finding it difficult to come up with some green cheese; but he is entertaining beyond compare and has a special way of keeping the atmosphere light and logical rather than weighting it with negative words. But if you try to share your problems with him, he'll have disappeared before you can blink twice.

He was born to inform you and to commune with you as he surprises you with his limitless array of new ideas. He will charm and entertain you with a never-ending supply of words and actions like the court jesters of Merry Old England. Although he's not likely to trudge through the ups and downs with you -- at least not without complaining loudly – he will surely lighten your load as he rides alongside cheering you on. Don't probe or question the reasons why he loves you; just let your love's laughter illuminate the shadows in your life and sparkle each new day with the joy that only a Geminian knows so well.

Mutable   **SAGITTARIUS**   **Fire**

ruler: Jupiter

A Sagittarian wants to be where-ever the action happens to be. Whether the action happens to be in the neighborhood or on the other side of the world, this happy-go-lucky troubador is sure to bounce in on all the goings-on. The world is his playground and he treats each continent as if it were his own backyard. You'll find this ad-venturer anywhere there's a chance to learn something totally new and different or to gather a group toget-her for a revival of the spirit.

Sagittarian guys have an easy and open manner. They get excited about the darndest things – among them, fast horses and beautiful women – or does it go the other way 'round? Sagittarian gals thrive on the adventure of people they've never met and places they've never been to before but only read about in school.

Gals are short on the patience of trivial duties like house-work and often find child rearing too demanding and con-fining, but they're good sports and a real asset on a two-week camp-out. Both guys and gals possess more than their share of a good sense of humor and can laugh at the drop of a participle. I'm not trying to say that the horse is all play and no work or all good times and no tears; the Sagittarian knows the meaning of sorrow as well as do the rest of us. He just tries to look over his miseries toward a brighter tomorrow.

Sagittarius is symbolized by the centaur, or creature whose head, trunk, and arms are those of a man; but whose body and legs are those of a horse. The symbol developed from Greek mythology, in which the centaur was a race of beings that dwelt in the mountains of Thessaly and Lapithae and were considered slaves to their animal passions.

Sagittarians are best known for their attempt to carry off the bride of Pirithous, son and successor of Ixion; hence, a battle amongst the kinsmen ensued. Centaurs are seen pulling the chariot of the god Dionysus and are often associated with strenuous physical activity, races, contests, wine, festivity, and amorous activity. They represent the inward struggle between barbarism and human reason.

Although mythological, centaurs were symbols of freedom of the spirit. Their home was in the wilderness and their passions reached beyond lust to a stable plateau in faith. So it is with the Sagittarian, who easily identifies with human failing but goes forth to inspire others to join him in his search for guidance from a higher source of knowledge.

Sagittarians have very warm and friendly eyes. Those eyes don't stand out in their appearence, but in the sparkly, friendly way that they look at you. Because the Sagittarian is a stranger to no one, his eyes will let you know you're included in what everyone else is doing, even though you may have just appeared on the scene.

Eyelashes are usually short, and the eyes are pale or yellow where they're supposed to be white; yet, they still sparkle most of the time. Eyebrows seem to grow here and there with abandon, although you may have to lift that shock of hair that's hanging in your horse's eyes, to find them.

Although horses have all types of noses, the classic Sagittarian nose has a prominent bridge high up near the forehead. That nose isn't especially broad or hooked, but the bridge protrudes so that many call it a Roman nose. I always call it a horse's nose. And when the horse is in a playful mood, he rubs his nose or scratches it with his arm or on his shoulder. He may also use his nose in expressing tenderness and love by rubbing it up and down on the cheeks, shoulders, and neck of the one he loves.

The horse's mouth is almost always doing something like chewing gum, munching potato chips, chewing his fingernails, and most often talking. His lips are generally full and sensuous, and he speaks with his mouth wide open so that you can see all the way back to his wisdom teeth as he pronounces some of the words he's saying or as he lets out a horse laugh. You'll see a lot of all of his teeth, for your Sagittarian subject smiles easily, and often. And as his smile turns into a grin, his eyes may even become a part of the show and may be squeezed into a squint. No one is capable of resisting a Sagittarian grin; it's definately contagious, and soon everyone in the room is smiling, too.

Although the shape of the face has many variations, the most obvious Sagittarian face is long with a pointed chin. Many whites sport a face full of freckles, especially in their youth.

Horses are easily annoyed with little things like hair cuts

and hair styles; therefore, the horse you've got in mind probably has her hair pulled back with a rubber bank or turned loose without pins, combs, or anything else that might hold it down. They prefer their hair's true color to anything artificial and consider hair oils and sprays unthinkable. Should you happen to find a filly with her hair all pinned up and sprayed down, you can bet she's all pinned down in her personal expression, too. Of course, occasional bursts of showiness at the starting gate – before the big race -- may occur from time to time.

Getting it straight from the horse's mouth brings in a wide range of tone and modulation. The voice pitches upward to dramatize the feelings of excitement and then down to express the closing points. There is always some hint of the evangelist in his voice.

Sagittarians blurt out their words regardless of whoever else happens to be talking and then trail off their own words in the middle of their own sentences because they've already thought of something else to say, or changed their minds.

While the horse is explaining his thoughts, he interjects

his phrases with little spurts of laughter or embellishes his ideas with foreign words. Because he's so proud of his education, he's likely to intersperse his words with quotations from all sorts of well-known sources, such as a well-respected professor or Solomon or Abraham Lincoln. Just when you've settled down and decided to listen instead of being interrupted again, he will shatter the quiet mood with his horse laugh.

The Sagittarian body shape is either long and leggy and built for running or somewhat shorter and stockier and built for pulling. If you were to measure the torso of the long, lean horse, you would probably find those bodies to be shorter than those of people whose total height is less. Long, lean horses are all legs and arms. Short draught horses are stocky and muscular with thick, solid arms and legs.

Gals often have wide hips and/or heavy thighs. It seems the wider their hips, the narrower are their legs from the knees to the ankles. Sagittarian women often have full bosoms but not until they're past their teens. Regardless of the body type, almost all horses stoop just a little.

The Sagittarian walk is bouncy and light. Lots of horses walk on the balls of their feet, applying heels only every two or three steps. Of course, that depends a lot on how fast they're going; and more often than not, they're running. They run up and down stairs, skipping steps as they go. They step over any-

thing that's in their way rather than to go around it.

Despite all these light steps mentioned, the horse is a clumsy sort who will trip over anything and everything within a two-foot radius of his path. He's a light dancer, especially on those fast steps; but you can expect to get your toes tromped.

Your first glance will show you the one with a heart as big as a breadbox and a mouth to match. He is kind and generous to every living thing but quick to extol his virtues to anyone who will listen. The horse is a laugh-a-minute as long as you're not the one everyone is laughing about. He is unruly looking, but he doesn't intend to look different from everyone else so that he can't be classed as a rebel. He wants to "do his own thing" and often takes too many shortcuts to his destination.

Horses eat just about anything and everything in sight with gusto and flair. They eat as though an invading army were just a few miles behind them, preferring food that can be taken with them as they run out the door. If you have a horse to feed, you'd be best off to cook lots of everything.

Needless to say, horses can overeat, allowing their appetites to take over their better judgments. Active horses won't be harmed by their gusty appetites as long as they stay on the go. The trouble is that those appetites stay on after the racing season is over and they've gone off to graze. A Sagittarian must apply steady caution about eating food that may attack the liver, such as rich sauces and gooey pastries. Over-consumption of alcohol can also be a problem.

Horses can stay slim and fit for years after youth by sticking to a diet of grains, fresh fruit, and nuts. They enjoy rare meat and other high protein food; in fact, they feel that anything that can be gathered in the wilderness is fair game.

In case you haven't guessed, horses are inclined to gain weight after their twenties. It seems that they are a skinny bag of bones until one day after about their thirtieth birthday they've discovered they need to diet!

The horse's clothing is nearly always sporty and outdoorsy. He could live in denim and high-top boots and sometimes look as though he's about to take off for the climb up Pike's Peak as soon as he gets off work. Even Sagittarian guys' suit coats often look like hunting jackets.

The Sagittarian gal prefers clothes with a casual look about them or suits with a military appearance. She may feel a little uncomfortable in fancy clothes designed for prim and proper ladies and dislikes the bother of most jewelry.

However, horses of both sexes are fond of big medallions that spell out their identity in a flash or of big rings that display their financial worth right out there where everyone can see it. Both guys and gals enjoy wearing scarves around their necks, big straw hats, and all sorts or boots. You may find your Sagittarian all decked out in a uniform - - the brighter the colors and the shinnier the buttons, the better.

Sagittarians are outdoorsy people and enjoy all sorts of strenuous activity. They like to "horse" around in an even contest or game by a roaring fire or to involve themselves in a seedy game of cards played in a smoke-filled room - - with money on each game, of course. They love horse racing and boxing matches and soap box derbies and turtle races; in fact, the only thing they don't like is to be left without a challenge, or to be left at home minding the kids while everyone else is out having fun.

They are restless students, especially those little colts of grammer-school age; but gradually they grow into their lessons when the instruction becomes philosophical. This occurs at about the middle teens. They're inclined to attend all sorts of programs in higher education and may change majors in university study just to stay in school or to keep from going to work.

Centaurs enjoy traveling almost as much as they enjoy eating and drinking and running and playing, and they enjoy nearly everything in life more than they enjoy working. They enjoy reading for the knowledge it provides, preferring books of a philosophical content. They are deeply respectful of the great masters and are inclined to quote any number of sources from Plato to Shakespeare and, of course, the Bible.

They are active in religion but are inclined to walk outside the confines of their earliest religious instruction. They may try out an assortment of religious disciplines as the years pass and may even change their religious basis drastically from Catholic to Protestant to Islam.

Sagittarians enjoy marriage to one who will sort out all that mountain of information and philosophical gleanings and make some sense of it. They enjoy sharing their thoughts through conversation and cherish one who will share the adventure of the unknown with them. Although the horse clings tenaciously to his freedom, he longs to have someone waiting there for him at the end of the day's race.

Security needs are met through living a life of virtue and self-denial - - by deeds that may go unrecognized by those around him; yet, he knows he has done his part in elevating mankind. His ultimate goals rest in his desire to be anaylitical and thorough, presenting a pristine-pure image to the world. Because his interests are often wider than they are deep, he strives to do the best possible job he can and to work as a part of a team.

The horse is often loud and braggish, among other annoyances. He is inclined to "blow" everything way out of proportion to the truth of the matter. He suffers from "hoof-and-mouth disease", stopping his mouth only long enough to change feet.

He wants to be an important part of whatever is going on and may promise to do more than his share of the work. You would be better off to check his track record before you put any money down on that horse, however. He may be arrogant and overbearing in his demeanor toward others when he feels superior to those around him, especially where his education is concerned.

He clings tenaciously to his freedom and makes a poor mate until maturity sets in, and this sometimes takes years and years. And alas, like so many world travelers since Man first embarked on foreign shores, he may have a girl in every port.

Sagittarians were born to inspire you and to encourage you to look up as you walk, away from the pins and buttons on the ground toward the stars and the vast expanse of the Universe. Should you be in love with a Sagittarian spectacle, your life will never be dull. They're here on this earth to entertain you, to love you - - if only for a little while - - and to hold your hand as you renew your faith in God.

Mutable   **VIRGO**   **Earth**

ruler: Mercury

A Virgoan needs to work and to serve others in order to feel important. Whenever there's nobody to help or nothing to do, these busy bees are busy tidying up or thinking of new ways to keep their hands occupied. You will find these energetic souls anywhere that they can clean up, sort out, and record.

Virgoan guys like to talk about their jobs. When they're not talking about work, they can be found puttering around the house or working on a hobby in the garage. They offer help willingly at the office or on the job and are inclined to serve others' egos even when they are aware of their own superiority.

Virgoan gals are workers, too, and take extra care to see to it that everyone under their wings is comfortable. Virgoan gals are easily found in the kitchen or the laundry room cleaning up after everyone else. But they make top-notch employees and are especially dependable about showing up on time.

Both guys and gals are naturals in health and medicine, believing that an ounce of prevention is worth a pound of cure.

Their senses of humor show them to be masters of the bad pun, which they inflict painfully into the conversation every few minutes.

Virgoans are usually well organized and place emotions carefully behind practicality and dependability. But they are not blind to the little favors others do for them, and each keeps an invisible checklist of friends and associates on whom he can depend.

Virgo is represented by the young woman, or virgin, gathering wheat in the field at harvest time. In keeping with the animal symbols, I would like to represent this sign with the symbol of the honeybee. The honeybee is a social insect that lives in a hive with other workers, a single queen and drones whose only task is to fertilize the queen.

At the height of the honeyflow, worker bees literally work themselves to death. As cold weather approaches, the drones are dumped from the hive and left to die. Honeybees work at an unceasing pace and cooperate with one another for the sake of their community, sharing and rearranging their tasks according to their capabilities.

Virgoans are among us to help bring order out of the chaos that surrounds us all. They thrive on work and work best in team efforts. A willingness to pitch in and share the load is evident in the face and manner of Virgo-rising people.

Just like the other three mutable signs – Gemini, Sagittarius, and Pisces, Virgo is an assortment of different features and characteristics that are difficult to pin down. Still, there will be certain features you can pick out, no matter how subtle.

A Virgoan face seems designed to "bite off" little bits of this and that; therefore, the crowded teeth will often catch your eye. The jawbone is too small to accommodate the teeth. Sometimes this feature is rather an outstanding one, as teeth are bucked or protruding in any number of ways.

To add to this feature, the mouth is often smaller in width than are the mouths of the other eleven signs. Even if it's not actually smaller, it seems so. The honeybee opens his mouth carefully, guarding the exit of words with tensed lips that purse easily and often. When he smiles, he seldom shows his teeth.

The chin is usually long, thin, and pointed. Even if the Virgoan's face is broad, the chin may be long and pointed. A three quarter view of Virgo's face may appear to lack contour. If this is not the case, it will be dramatically bony and angular with high cheekbones.

In either case the silouette will be significant. And last but not lease, when none of the above rules apply, you will be able to pick out a Virgoan ascendant by a jawbone that protrudes at a near ninety degree angle from the neck.

The eyes of all the mutable signs are their least noticeable feature: the honeybee is no exception. As previously mentioned, the mutable signs may take on the characteristics of the other signs by combination according to their charts or by taking on the characteristics of the sign in which Virgo's ruler, Mercury, is placed.

Rather than depend on the physical appearance of the eyes, look for the soft, gentle willing-worker look. A Virgoan needs to receive lots of approval from everyone around him, and his eyes are his big giveaway. Eyes almost plead for permission to exist, like the puppy who comes to your door asking whether he can sleep by the stove for a little while. Eyebrows lack organization and may require some care for neatness -- a Virgo must.

The nose takes on a lot of different appearances, too; but there's a higher than average chance that it will have a large protruding bridge, especially on whites. Despite all that nose room, your Virgoan subject may have sinus trouble. He is sensitive to foods and pollen and suffers especially during hay-fever season. Even so, he's probably a smoker.

A Virgoan has hair that is neat, clean, and almost always combed to perfection. When it's not "neat as a pin," it stands out in its wild, unkempt condition. There's seldom any in-between.

Virgoan gals favor pinning their hair in stylish or librarian-like buns and twists on top of their heads. Short-haired bees wear their hair in simple fashion, cut to be washed and combed without the mess of pins and curlers, somewhat like short-haired Geminian gals, only even shorter and plainer.

Virgoans are careful when they talk and use caution in keeping their reputations spotless. For this reason, they hesitate before, during, and after almost all of their sentences and then apologize for having given any sort of unconventional statement, no matter how mild. The larger their audience, the more timid and embarrassed will be the Virgoan speaker. He will cough and clear his throat, backtrack, repeat, and apologize for having offended anyone when he is through. On the light side, his phrases are interspersed with light, harmless humor and corny puns -- that special Virgo trademark. Although he is shy, he enjoys instructing others and often talks like a school teacher.

The Virgoan body shape emphasizes an ability to work at either physical or secretarial duties. The short, stocky Virgoan looks as if he is capable of working a dawn-to-dark schedule at various agricultural chores, the primary function of its

symbol, the wheatgatherer. His legs are especially stocky and muscular. The ankles are thick and strong.

Long, lean Virgoans look as if they should be posed with pens, waiting to jot down each word uttered by the most important person in the room. These secretarial Virgoans may remind you of the scribes kings used to have with them at all times, keeping records of incoming slaves and gold. They have especially long fingers and oversized ears.

Virgo-rising people gradually develop protruding abdomens as the years mount up. This becomes apparent by the mid-thirties and has little to do with overweight. They almost always slouch just a little; thus, a pouchy tummy is sometimes the result of the body's contour. Parents of Virgoan teens might just as well give up trying to correct junior's posture and simply blame it on the sign.

The Virgoan step is a gentle scuffle. He doesn't want to draw attention to himself and he doesn't want to make a mess. She doesn't want to click her heels because her mother told her when she was a little girl that it wasn't lady-like. Therefore, Virgoans walk softly but firmly, making sure each footstep is securely planted before proceeding. Despite the soft step, the Virgoan stands so securely that he seems to be rooted to the spot. Picture your subject swinging a scythe, and you have the idea.

Virgoans have sensitive digestive systems and suffer indigestion whenever things aren't going well in their lives. They are health-food freaks and stress vitamin pills and nutrition but sometimes make too much of it, treating their diets like a religion. Like the honeybee, they store up lots of food in the pantry to be eaten on cold winter days. They enjoy growing their own food organically if they have garden space. They are outspoken about others' eating habits when it's none of their business. Likewise, they often preach about the way alcohol kills brain cells and how food preservatives affect the nervous system.

A Virgoan often identifies himself with his clothing. He probably has a large wardrobe, although many of his clothes closely resemble one another. He wears clothes designed to attract the least amount of attention to himself. Although his clothing may be fashionable, it won't stand out as a fore-runner of next year's scene. Whether in blue jeans or a tweed suit, a Virgoan is neat and tidy with his collar buttoned and his necktie straight, despite the high summer temperatures.

She's careful about looking unladylike and keeps her hemlines at the exact fashion length of the season partly to attract less attention and to dress correctly. Guys don jackets at all business and social functions, especially where ladies are present.

The absent-minded professor type Virgoan is sometimes careless about missing buttons on his jackets and gravy stains on his ties. Even so, you probably won't catch him in his shirtsleeves unless he's alone in his office or talking things over with his peers. He dresses according to his position at work and out of respect to his superiors.

As a form of recreation, Virgo-rising people often pursue work as an after-hours activity. They "moonlight" because work is their most natural means of expression. Second jobs also fill their desire to be in the action – bartending at a Singles Club, teaching in the Adult Education Program, filling in at the local bookstore or dress shop, or docking boats on the lake. They seem to feel guilty just having fun for the sake of having fun.

Sports that emphasize health and opportunities for relaxation are attrative to a Virgoan; but he favors activities in which he can combine work with pleasure, such as gardening. Because his health is so important to him, he is attracted to yoga and exercise workouts. He enjoys owning small pets and may raise them for profit.

A Virgoan enjoys marriage for the unpredictability and sensitivity it brings into his otherwise orderly, insensitive life. He favors one who always retains a bit of mystery and is especially fascinated by those who are clairvoyant and whose faith is a guiding force, for the Virgoan's common sense can get to be a drag even to himself sometimes.

Honeybees expect the one with whom they share their lives to be neat, tidy, and clean above all else! Because a Virgoan is seldom demonstrative with his feelings, he must find a mate who is able to intuit his feelings.

Security needs are met through associates who are honorable and admirable, for a Virgoan doesn't lie and expects others not to do so. He thrives on philosophy although he seldom really understands it, and on a belief that he is following the Divine Plan.

He is easily defeated by discouraging words and easily inflated with pride when he is lauded by those whom he respects. Ultimate goals are attained through the knowledge gained for its usefullness, as well as for its own sake. The Virgoan gathers knowledge about him on as many different topics as he can digest, considering it his birthright to pass that knowledge on to others. He makes a good teacher on all topics, as well as does he possess a knack for writing.

Fussy, picky mannerisms and critical remarks are the honeybee's most annoying characteristics. Although others may turn a deaf ear to tid-bits of gossip, the Virgoan picks up every fragment, especially if the gossip concern's someone's promiscuous behavior.

He is sensitive and overly concerned about what the neighbors will think; and while he is listening to you, he will flick and pick off every hair and piece of lint on his clothing or fidget with the crumbs on the table. He's better at taking orders than in giving them and has some difficulty expressing originality. He may care a great deal for you but will allow others's opinions to interfere with his own, permitting the relationship to break up if the gossip gets too thick around you.

Occasionally, a Virgoan acts more like a drone than a worker, feeling his sole task is to produce lots more little ones like himself. Because he retains the critical view toward the rest of the world, he cannot see the forest for the tree of sanctimonious virtue that stands squarely in his view. He somehow manages to retain a feeling of purity and well being, despite his behavior.

Virgoans aren't concerned about feelings; they just want to know the facts. If there's a job to be done, they'll do it. They will clean and care for you, anxiously bringing you a second cup of coffee while they dust away the crumbs around your saucer and listen patiently to your daily woes without divulging a whisper of their own.

They were born to serve you and to maintain an element of calm and a keen sense of proportion in this tormented sea we call life. They won't openly defend you or inspire you with great amounts of courage and daring, but they will shelter you in private if they think your ambitions are worthy. And they will love you the only way Virgoans know how to love, and that is by respecting and admiring everything for which you stand.

Mutable   **PISCES**   **Water**

Ruler: Neptune

(Old ruler, Jupiter)

Pisceans need to sacrifice themselves in the name of other people
or things in order to feel worthy
of their own existence. Should
your Piscean subject happen to
demonstrate a strong will, it's
not because of his fishy ascendant
but because of the placement and
aspects between the planetary
indicators in his chart. You will
find these gentle poets anywhere
that they can inspire others to
look for a higher source of power
and energy than in the everyday
dilemmas to which most of us are bound.

Piscean guys are sensitive and sympathetic. They try to help everyone in the whole world by ridding this burdened planet of misery, hunger and disease. They're inclined to be worrisome and paranoid without apparent reason.

Piscean gals are even more sensitive, feeling so deeply at times that you may think they're acting out a part in a Greek Tragedy. Both guy and gal Pisceans may devote a lifetime to a hopeless cause: an unworthy mate, a dependent parent, or a profession that shows no promise. They stick with their hopeless causes because in their own minds their problems will all work out someday.

They sometimes have difficulty dealing with reality, but they are kind and considerate beyond human limits, taking more than their share of abuse from others. The Piscean isn't here to demand, to insist, or to control Mankind but rather to make this world more beautiful and to make us more aware of each other's needs.

Pisces is symbolized by two fish swimming in opposite directions. Maybe it's symbolic in itself that these two fish that represent Pisces aren't any particular kind of fish but just fish. (Today ichthyologists are familiar with more than 20,000 species of true fishes.)

Although some fish are fierce fighters and are considered good game fish to fishermen, many or most other species fall into less aggressive categories. The flounder, for instance, can be pulled up on the hook without resistance. Fish live in water all their lives, reproducing by either eggs or by bearing their young alive. At the advent of birth, both mother and father, as well as the rest of their community, devour many of their young.

Pisceans were meant to guide the rest of us toward peace and selflessness. They are more sensitive than we to sights, sounds, smells, and the vibrations of our universe. This awareness usually shows clearly in the face and manner of those with Pisces rising.

Although I've mentioned this before, the mutable signs don't follow a predictable pattern as a rule. Their moods and mannerisms are more apparent; yet, there are some facial characteristics that will stand out. Of these, the Piscean mouth creates that gentle smile that is so pure and unblemished that you will be temporarily (or permanently) mesmerized.

Although they don't smile often, when the fish are so inclined, their smiles will touch your heart. Most of the time, however, the Piscean mouth is turned downward in a sad, clown-like frown. Thy don't always smile when they're amused. Instead, they smile when the burdens of life have been temporarily lifted from their shoulders. A times, the Piscean mouth may show the reflection of the Virgoan polarity, revealing crowded and protruding teeth.

Remember the Irish ballad "When Irish Eyes are Smiling..?" Just replace the words "Irish" with "Pisces" and you have it. Surely, it's like the mornin' dew with a look of gentle innocence that will urge you to slay dragons in his defense.

The eyelids are droopy, and he looks as though he's just gotten out of bed. Whatever you do, don't try to awaken a

Fish: he won't fight back or be jarred into reality; he'll just swim away to a more comfortable part of the lake.

Sometimes the fish look like Librans; I don't know why, but they do. The only way to figure out which is which is to note whether your subject has an aggressive or a passive manner. The nose often takes on Libran characteristics with a crease right down the middle. More often, the nose will either be thick and fleshy -- a water sign trait -- or it will have a Virgoan appearance, because of the polarity of the signs, with a large protruding but bony bridge.

The Piscean chin slants inward toward the neck and has a dimple in it. Some might call it a "weak" chin. There's a little bulge of fat underneath commonly known as a double chin that helps make up for the lack of chin on the face. Cheeks are sometimes full looking as if they could carry extra food in them, the way chipmunks do. As old age creeps up, these cheeks tend to sag, and it is not uncommon to see an elderly fish with a face that's wider at the bottom than it is at the top.

Should a Piscean go this way or that? The two fish are swimming in opposite directions; thus, your Piscean subject

usually doesn't know which way to go or how he really feels about things. He'll readily go along with the crowd.

His head tips from side to side in either conversation or thought. He might begin to say something and then withdraw the words before they are uttered. He's afraid to make waves, or else he's changed his mind in the time lapse from when the thought first occured to him. He seems to be saying "oh, woe is me" as he wrinkles his forehead and looks pensively toward the floor. The fish's forehead bears the lines of worry and frustration, just as the lines on either side of his mouth appear prominent.

Piscean hair may be soft and silky or wild, dull, unkempt and wiry. In fact, it's more likely to be either or those examples than any of the broad spectrum of possibilities in between. Sometimes this diversity of appearance can be found on the same fish at different times of the week.

Fish are inclined to forget about such things as haircuts and trips to the barber shop or to the beauty parlor and may allow the roots of their hair to grow out dark (or light) on a dyed or bleached head. Sometimes they try to imitate a

fashionable hairstyle that looks absolutely dreadful on them, but they don't realize it because they see only what they want to see. On the other hand, their hair may be their most alluring asset. A beautiful Piscean woman may remind you of a mermaid -- too beautiful to be real.

The Piscean voice is either soft and dreamy or whiny and overflowing with self-pity. The same fish may swim from one manner of speech to the other within a short span of time, depending on the point he is trying to get across.

At other times, the Piscean voice is filled with so much gentle persuasion that you're caught before you know what's hooked you. On rare occasions a Piscean is inclined to preach, attempting to inspire his audiences with hope, or hell and damnation.

The Piscean body shape places emphasis on the hands and feet. Both hands and feet are noticeable in their expressiveness. Hands move about effortlessly as the fish moves his fins, but the feet are often clumsy and awkward. Fish, after all, belong in the water, not on land.

The midsection takes on extra pounds easily, leaving those long arms and legs to retain their slimness. The fish's body fills out easily in the face and neck. Double chins can reach an enormous size. The skin is both sensitive and easily stretched so that once excess weight has come about, the skin is likely to retain its inflated dimensions even though the Piscean has returned to normal size again. Fish have thin skin that easily reacts to a sensitivity to their diets -- or to embarrassment shown by blushing.

Fish walk so softly that you will hardly hear them coming. They even limp quietly. They slide along gently, watching out for obstacles that must be detoured. There is a greater than average possibility that Pisceans will walk with a limp because of foot ailments or that one of the feet will turn in toward the other. Fish are outstanding dancers when they want to be, however, as long as they don't have to move too quickly. Their feet ooze gently across the floor and the fish is ever fretful that he will step on your toes.

Your first glance will show you the dreamy soul who hides behind a mask of fantasy and make believe. Pisceans aspire to a kind of greatness that reaches beyond the clouds of human capability; yet, they quickly settle for a tenement dwelling and a welfare check while they wait patiently for their ship to come in to port. They work out their unhappiness

through painting, singing, poetry and prayer, or by gently chuckling "oh well, it'll all work out OK tomorrow." On the other hand, they view happiness and the good times with suspicion and some dismay.

Pisceans eat frequently -- too frequently sometimes. There seems to be a need to put something into their mouths more often than their bodies require nourishment. They like to drink sweet things or alcoholic beverages, to chew candy and gum, and to smoke.

They also feel that there is some magical property to anything in pill form, and they can be found grabbing the aspirin bottle upon the slightest hint of anxiety. They enjoy eating fish and all seafood and should make special efforts to avoid heavy fatty foods or sweets, for they are highly sensitive to sugar.

Fish wear clothes that add to the illusion of mystery and the intrigue about them when they are feeling high. But when they are feeling low down you'll probably find them in tattered rags and general disarray. Pale gray suits or neatly fitting sports clothes are favorites on Piscean guys. Gals allure in filmy, flowing dresses with big sleeves.

Both guy and gal fish enjoy bright, splashy flowered prints and stripes and glimmery, shimmery fabric. You're likely to find your Piscean subject in swimwear if it's at all possible. They spend large amounts of money on their shoes and may be required to wear orthopedic shoes because of foot ailments.

Pisceans enjoy sitting quietly, doing as little as possible. They're dreamers, mystics, poets and artists; but they're not inclined to involve themselves in very much physical activity. The single exception to that is their fondness for almost all water activity. You probably won't find them competing in speed boat races -- they'll leave that for their neighbor, Ariens. But they do enjoy swimming, sailing, and fishing, of course. When they're not around water, they can be found creating pictures with a brush or pen. They are excellent photographers, favoring scenes of wildlife or natural beauty.

Pisceans are natural healers and are often found in hospitals, nursing homes, and institutions for the crippled or the elderly. They may also be found in prisons or detention centers. Many are gifted in the art of psychic healing. And because they are easily inspired by the Word of God, they can be found caring for social rejects in skid row missions or giving their time at homes for orphans, stray animals and juvenile delinquent homes. They are natural clairvoyants, psychomotrists, and readers of almost everything from cards to tea leaves.

Pisceans lean heavily on those around them and seek out loved ones who will make many of their decisions for them. They don't enjoy being single and alone unless they're the hermit type, in which case they don't like to be around anybody. The average fish is highly dependent and may even become a clinging vine. They try to do all they can to make their partners happy, as a rule, but need lots of praise and flattery to avoid discouragement.

Security needs are met through sound communication with those whom they love and respect and through knowledge gained by reading from the great sources of wisdom, such as the Bible. Pisceans seek a religious plateau and a place in the world as a leader of the souls of men as their ultimate goals of achievement. They find lasting joy in securing converts to their religious beliefs and hope to be remembered as prophets in centuries to come.

Your fish is easily victimized by the cunning of others or simply by his need to be a martyr. He may find an unhealthy pleasure in being used as a doormat or being imprisoned within the confines of a detrimental relationship. Oddly enough, your Piscean friend or loved one may care only too much for the miseries of those homeless waifs in a distant portion of the globe though he cares too little about the personal tragedies of friends and loved ones.

He doesn't wish to get involved; thus, it's easier to suffer with the starving Chinese than to get emotionally involved with an anxious loved one. They can create a scene around themselves with the flavor of an oldtime melodrama and then somehow become the victim of the plot.

They are inclined to express their personalities through their illnesses and always have a ready supply of new ailments to replace the old ones. They often lean heavily on their children, expecting them to make most of their decisions for them.

Your Piscean subject will probably never be recognized for his logic and good sense but for his gentleness, sensitivity, and willingness to accept all that you offer him.

Pisceans barely whisper their own ideas in fear of backlash or rejection; yet, they seem to know more about the universe and its workings than any of the rest of us will ever fully comprehend. They were born to soften and to beautify your life and to guide you toward the invisible, unexplainable forces that you may not comprehend; yet, you know these forces are there. Should you be fortunate enough to be loved by a Piscean, your love will carry your dreams beyond the most distant star; for you see, your Piscean love already knows the way up there.